WORTHY

Alicia Rose
XOXO
To: Susan,
you are worthy

Alicia Rose

ISBN 978-1-0980-7385-5 (paperback)
ISBN 978-1-0980-8192-8 (hardcover)
ISBN 978-1-0980-7386-2 (digital)

Christian Faith Publishing, Inc.
832 Park Avenue
Meadville, PA 16335
www.christianfaithpublishing.com

Printed in the United States of America

To my mom, thank you for fighting for us to have a better life. To my dad, Chuck, thank you for being our north star. I love you both more than you know. To Jeremy, my rock, I love and adore you. To Jackson, without you, I would have never started this journey. You are my why. I love you, kid. And last but certainly not least, to my "Mamow Lowis." Lord, have mercy. How I love you.

Introduction: Worthy

Well, hello, sisters. I am really excited that you're holding my book right now. I know how precious your time is, and I can promise you that this book is my heart and soul in the paper. The single purpose of this book is to inspire you to realize how amazing you are, how you already have everything inside of you that you need to be happy. There will be stories that will hopefully make you laugh and possibly make you cry and realize that you're not alone. In this world of filters and competition, I'm coming to you as myself. Now don't get me wrong, this girl loves good mascara and hair extensions like nobody's business, but I'm no longer putting a Band-Aid on a deeper wound. I've learned that we must heal from the inside out. Not the outside in. It just does not work that way. We can go around and around that issue for as long as we have to, but we can't pass go until we learn. I needed to embrace my past, face my fears, and be really honest with myself. Anxiety, depression, feelings of not being good enough were stuffed so deeply inside me that I was starting to resemble the Stay Puft Marshmallow Man. I'm certain that you can do the same thing and embrace who you are apologetically. That, my friend, is what freedom feels like. Come and be free with me! You're worth the work. Fight for the best version of you. I hope at the end of this book; you feel as though you have always known me, like an old best friend. Hopefully, bearing the parts of my life that weren't so pretty can inspire you to realize that the past has no hold on what the future can bring.

Chapter 1

Chasing the Mirage

Have you ever felt that you are always chasing something? For example, "I'll be happy when we buy a house." Then it turns into, "I'll be happy when we're all moved into said house." Then it's, "I'll be happy when the house is remodeled." Then when that's to our satisfaction, we're on to something else. That's what I did. So instead of enjoying the journey with my husband, I felt constantly frustrated and overwhelmed. I wish I could have told the old me, "Enjoy the journey, and eating from your old '70s counter top will someday be a good memory in the part of your journey."

I know far more about this than I should, mainly because I've chased a mirage most of my life. I was trying to chase something down that would fill that sense of longing or completeness. It's a lot easier to find a quick fix for your problems than it is to dig deep, rip off the scab, and get to work. It's hard work, but it's work that needs to be done. Then once it's done, we can continue with life in its wholeness. Not always searching for the next thing to feel better temporarily. Before I began this journey of inner work, I circled the same mountain over and over again. I could not pass until I worked through my issues. I would always end up in the same spot time after time.

As a child, I had a pretty colorful childhood. It was full of love, happiness, sadness, crazy stories, loss, and restoration. Let me share my story with you. Our God is in the restoration business, and this is my story of how He restored me.

I was born in 1985 in Barbourville, Kentucky. It was a hot, muggy Southern day, I was told. My mom and dad brought me home to a little house deep in the "Holler." So my story began. My mom is one of the toughest women I've ever known. She takes no crap and can make just about anything beautiful. My dad, who has since passed, was a fun guy. He was a friend to everyone but a terrible husband. He had issues that he never worked through, resulting in drug use and becoming an alcoholic. He was extremely abusive to my mom. His temper was so explosive it was like a volcano ready to erupt at any time. He was a pot farmer, and believe it or not, we lived in a dry county, so alcohol sales were prohibited. So he became a bootlegger. We had this cool barn, and he made one of the stalls the beer room. People would drive up and tell him if they wanted a six-pack or a twelve-pack. If they answered six-pack, he would get his X-Acto knife out and cut it in half. They would pay and be on their way. This is how he made his living. We lived on fifty acres or so of land. There was a beautiful stream that winded through.

My aunt Judy lived across the field with my cousins Michelle and David; she and mom were best friends. Mom said she was the closest thing to a sister that she ever had. She was like another parent to me as well. Her husband, which was my uncle Earl, would go out drinking with my dad. They would both come home in the same state—hungry, broke, and ready to fight. Now, my aunt Judy had some nerve pills. Those two ladies soon figured how which pill was "undetectable" ground inside a tuna fish sandwich. When they would pass out, they would take the money that they didn't already blow, and they would happily craft and enjoy a day or two of quiet. When they would wake up, they wouldn't remember much, and they would think that they spent all their money. Now those women had moxie. *Moxie*, I love that word. I love what it means. *Moxie*—the force of character, determination, or nerve. Down the road, the other direction was my uncle John, aunt Debbie, and my cousins Nikki, Trampus, Will, and Little John. Their house was always fun and filled to the brim with kids. Uncle John was so special to me. He was my father's older brother, and he always tried to help him and give him guidance. He was a rock for the entire family; he is greatly missed as well as Aunt Judy.

My other uncle David lived a few minutes away near the Little Store; the Little Store was a tiny gas station. We frequented it so much that we had a tab, and my father would pay it off once a month. My uncle David is a good, kind man. He is a family man and always had a good head on his shoulders.

My grandma, a.k.a. Mamow, was lovely; she and I were very close. She was about 110 pounds of love and food-making fury. She was always cooking. That was her love language. My uncle John told me that his mom (Mamow) would pack him a Herman Munster lunch box filled with enough food to feed an army when he was in school. My grandpa Will had died before I was born; she loved him so much and always talked about him. She called him Big Red; he was a coal miner. Grandma worried, smoked cigarettes, and drank coffee, and then worried some more. She would often say, "Lord, have mercy. I'm going to have a nervous breakdown." When I was a little girl, around five or six years, I prayed for God not to let Grandma have a nervous breakdown. She is also where I got the phrase "hankering for a cookie." That went over well with my family in Indiana (Inset eye roll and sigh.)

They still call me Corn Bread.

My father would go out on drinking binges and return after a couple of days in a rage. He would beat my mom and tear apart the house. Once, he threw everything my mom owned into the creek. I would scream for him to stop, but he wouldn't listen. I can still see the look in his eyes when he would do it. His eyes would look like a scared deer. Our haven was Aunt Judy's house; Mom would have me run out the side door and go to her house for safety. He would never hit me, but the trauma of seeing my mom beaten was hard. Mom would run out behind me as soon as she could get away. One night, in particular, I remember us running away to Aunt Judy's house. My cousin Michelle was not home, and we got into her bed. My mom begged me to be quiet; we heard the front door open, and he came looking for us. The bedroom door was open a tiny crack, and I remember watching him. Aunt Judy convinced him that we weren't there. He left, and we went to sleep. The next morning was a school day. Mom let me stay home because my voice was hoarse from screaming the night before; I can't imagine how painful that was for her to see her child go through that.

Since our house wasn't very safe for me, I spent a lot of time with my Mamow; we would eat Jack's Pizzas and drink RC Cola; dessert would, of course, be a moon pie or four moon pies. Grandma's love language was food, remember? I would go down to the Piggly Wiggly with her and get these little fruit pies. They were fried in lard. Why is lard so delicious? Friends, I kid you not when I tell you that she put lard in everything. Grandma could really cook; she could fry cornbread like nobody's business. Heart problems were a common occurrence in our family. I'd have to say it's the eating habits; clogged arteries are no joke. Nothing feels more comforting to me than a good fried meal, though, all health consciousness aside. That must be embedded deep in my psyche, in my early memories of comfort.

I would play in the creek that curled around our property; it was my little swimming pool. I would play with Barbies, and to my mother's horror, I once caught baby copperhead snakes in her mixing bowl.

We had a sheep named Rambow. He was a major jerk. He would charge at you with his head down and knock you flat on your back. We lived in the "Holler." For those of you that may not know what that is, it's the low place between two mountains. When you would look around, all you would see are mountains. At night, it was very dark, and there were no streetlights. We didn't have a garage, so when we would come home at night, you would hope, pray, and book it to the door as fast as you could before Rambow would come and send you flying through the night sky. My mom got the wiser of him and decided to tie a bell around his neck, so now you had a warning of Rambow's approach. So, going into the house went more like this: open the car door, listen for the bell (Okay, no bell), get out of the car, and walk toward the house. What, what's that? That's a bell! Panic sets in, and you hear the bell getting louder and ringing faster and faster. You try to guess which direction it's coming, and hopefully, you make it to the door before Rambow makes it to you. How do sheep have such good eyesight? Is that a thing? Once that I remember, probably many times, my poor mom had to get on top of the car to get away from the disgruntled sheep. Now mind you, we didn't sheer the sheep and make mittens from the wool. We just had a big jerk of a sheep because my father brought him home one day. We also had a mean duck named Quacker Doo; we got them as a pair, and the other one drowned in his water dish. I always assumed Quacker Doo was mean because he missed his friend.

On Fridays, Mom and I would go to the dollar store, and she would tell me that I could get anything that I wanted; this would consist of a baby doll or anything of that nature. From the time I can remember, all I ever wanted to do was be a mom. I would dress up my dolls and get real bottles and real clothes. I didn't want doll clothes. I wanted the real thing. It's hard to believe that we only have one child. After the store, we would go to Subway and get a cold cut combo with green onions and black olives—with oil and vinegar to finish it off. To this day, that's still what I eat.

My Dad and I would ride around in his black Silverado truck and listen to country music. As we would walk out the door, Mom would say, "Mark, don't be drinking and driving with Alicia in the car." Sadly that's another thing that I thought was normal. We would always stop by "the little store," I would get a mountain dew and Reese's peanut butter cup. I would sign the tab. We would drive around to visit his friends. He would call it loafin'. We would drive house to house until we would find a friend that was home. They would call me boss. If I were lucky, there would be some kids to play with. He would hand out beer and drink. I would run around the countryside playing with whoever was available. When we would get hungry, we would invade the nearest woman's kitchen and get a sandwich. When I was a kid in Kentucky, the women rarely worked, at least the ones I knew. They were homemakers and took care of the children. Always prepared to feed whatever group of children that were there, theirs or not. Southern hospitality is real; it's deeply embedded in me, and for that, I am grateful. Come over anytime, come hungry, and let me take care of you. That is also my love language. Bring your children and let them be at home. I'll show them where I keep the cookies. Sometimes my dad would drink too much, and I would have to help him steer his truck. I started to do this probably around age five. I thought it was fun, but for him, it was a necessity.

My mom had decided to get a night job; whatever money Dad would make, he would drink it up or spend it on who knows what. Mom always wanted a better life for me, and she fought hard for it. She thought that if she could work while we were sleeping, all would be well. One night my father decided to take me over to his friend's house with him; they had kids there, and the wife's name was Lorrie. I liked her so much; she was also a friend to my mom. So I had a great time playing, and as time went by, it got later and later. I can't tell you what time it was, but my father came in and said, "It's time to go home." I had fallen asleep with the other kids, and I had woke up when I heard him. He could barely walk and was hanging on to the wall. Laurie stepped in and said, "Just let her stay here and sleep. Come get her tomorrow." As a mother now, I knew what she was doing; she kept me safe and was a good friend to my mom. My father made it home. How? I don't know. He had passed out cold. My mom comes home from work, and she can't find me. She couldn't wake him up; she didn't know where I was. She took off going around to find me; now, this was before cell phones, and we didn't have a house phone. My poor mama. She found me at Laurie's house. She quit her job after that day. I would have done the same thing myself.

My life felt normal to me; it's all that I knew. I thought all men hit their wives. I thought that dads not working was normal; strife was normal for me. Screaming and yelling was just a way of life. I would be at school and be daydreaming as kids do. I would not be thinking about what cool thing I was going to do when I got home. I would be wondering if my mom was okay, hoping that she wouldn't be beaten and crying when I got off the bus.

Little did we know that things were going to be changing. God had other plans for us. He had plans for prosperity and a future; it would be quite a difficult road ahead. There is always a preparation period, and we must walk through that to have the reward.

Chapter 2

A New Shower Stall and New Life

My grandparents from Indiana were coming down to visit us. Mom told me the news, and I sat on our brown couch—you know, the one with wagon wheels on it that everyone in the '80s had? It also had the wooden arms you were likely to knock yourself out if you jumped on it wrong. Well, I sat on it and looked out the window for hours. For a seven-year-old girl, time really goes slow when you're excited. They are my mom's parents. My grandpa had a mobile home repair business and could repair just about anything. Mom had wanted a new shower stall. When they finally arrived, we were so excited to see them!

They gave me Life Savers—funny what you remember, isn't it? We visited and had a good time. Grandpa worked hard and put in the new shower stall. It looked really nice. Mom was so excited to have it done. She always took great pride in her home.

We decided to go out to dinner; my father wasn't home at that time, and once again, we had no cell phones. What a beautiful invention the cell phone is. We didn't know where he was, so we went off without him. When we got back home, what we found would change the whole trajectory of our life. He had come home while we were gone; he had found an empty house. He thought that we had left for good. He went into a rage and shot holes in our house and the brand-new shower stall and trashed our house.

Mom was instantly in tears, and my grandparents were so shocked at what they saw. I started to cry as well. As I am writing this, my son is seven years old; it seems as though this was a lifetime ago for me—almost like it wasn't my life. It was very much, though. I was standing in my room, and my mom came in to talk to me. She asked me if I wanted to leave and go to Indiana with Grandma and Grandpa. She said we wouldn't be able to come back for a long time. I said yes; she went and got some trash bags. She told me to put everything I wanted in them as quickly as I could. We all knew what trouble was around the corner if my father pulled into the driveway. We didn't even have to say it out loud. There were many times he had shot at her. He once shot at her as she was pulling out of the driveway, and I was in the car with her. She kept yelling for me to get on the floorboard. So I quickly took my favorite toys and stuffed them into the bags. Mom emptied my drawers of clothing into the bags as well.

My grandparents helped Mom load the car and get anything big that she wanted; it was around Christmastime, and they had brought down gifts. I was getting a TV for my room and was so excited. Once the car was loaded, we all got in, including my hamster Barney. I said, "We have to say bye to Mamow." Mom said, "We can't; your dad may be there." Then came more tears. I was devastated to leave her; it still makes me cry twenty-four years later as I'm writing this. As we drove away, I had no idea what our new life would be like.

As an adult, I can look in retrospect and see that my mom's tears weren't just from leaving the life she knew and fear of change. It was what she had to face to save me. She had a very traumatic childhood, filled with verbal and physical abuse. She had to walk right into her childhood trauma to save me from mine.

We lived with my grandparents until Mom could get on her feet. They have a big white two-story house; it was very pretty, with a huge yard with lots of flowers and a pool. My uncles worked for my grandpa's business so that they would be over every morning before work. Grandma would make us bacon and eggs. I would go off to school, and they would go off to work. Mom quickly found a factory job. She worked extremely hard, often seventy hours a week; she was so strong.

So let me set the tone here. I'm starting in the middle of the school year as a first-grader in a new school, with an accent so thick that you could cut it with a butter knife. I stutter, have a big gap in my teeth—thank goodness that thing closed up. I could drink through a straw without opening my mouth. Kinda weird, but it's the truth. I also used words like *hankering* and said, "Lord have mercy." I knew every word of every country song of the late '80s and early '90s. My dream was to be a country singer like Reba McEntire. I wanted to wear flashy sequin dresses and be on the stage under the bright lights. Let's just say I was a little different from the other girls. During this time, some awesome humans created the Shake 'n Bake commercial. Thank you, awesome humans. For those of you that don't know what that is, I'll enlighten you. You should still google it and watch the clip because it's worth it. Trust me. So it's a black-and-white commercial, and this little Southern girl comes in and says, "It's Shake 'n Bake, and I helped," as she shakes the bag of chicken. It's kinda ironic that I have a couple of boxes of that in our pantry. I still make Shake 'n Bake. It's just good.

So there were a certain few girls that were not very nice to me. Guess what they called me? Yep, you got it. They called me "Shake'n

Bake" and "Kentucky fried chicken." My uncle Scott started the nickname "Corn Bread." He actually yelled, "Go, Corn Bread," when I graduated high school. When I got my first car, he wanted to get a vanity plate that said *cornbread*; my mom wouldn't let him. Thank you, Mom. I didn't know this at the time, but my hometown was where the actual first Kentucky Fried Chicken restaurant was located. It's still up and running, and they have a museum located inside the restaurant. I went back to visit a couple of years ago, and I took a picture next to the sign. My cousins Nikki, Ann, her daughter, and Jackson, ate there before we went home from our trip. That meal was the last gift from my uncle John. That's a whole 'another story that I'll get into later. I had gone full circle. I was proud to be from Kentucky; I wish I still had my accent because hearing my Southern cousins talk sounds so pretty to me. I was proud to be a Southern girl even though I had been removed for so many years. These were my roots and my first memories. I still have a playlist of country music from that era, and it's comforting to me.

So, this girl did not fit in. I had been plucked from the hills of Kentucky and dropped in a very northern place, where they ate, spoke, dressed, and even thought differently. One was not right or wrong, just different. I adapted but longed for my home in Kentucky. Mainly my grandma, the toys that I left behind. I longed not to stick out like a sore thumb and be ridiculed. Somewhere along the line, I went from knowing who I was and marching to the beat of my drum to being weird. I don't hold any grudge against those "mean girls"; they had no clue what I was going through. I may not have such compassion for the underdog, the broken, the sad, the left out if it wasn't for them. They helped me cultivate my love language.

Life was pretty settled, and we got into a good routine. I got to talk to my father, grandma, aunts, uncles, and cousins on the phone. Mom had filed for divorce, and she was going through a terrible custody battle. She was trying to prove that he was an unfit parent, which was the truth; he loved me, but he wasn't fit to be responsible for a child. She allowed him to come up and see me; she never tried to keep me from him. She was trying to keep me from his sole care at any time. It didn't work, though. The courts would not rule in her favor. She always had full custody, but he got visitation rights. Since we were so far away, every other weekend was out of the question. I had to go down for a month each summer. This tore my poor mom apart. She had my mamow promise that I would never be alone with him. She promised, and just like that, summer vacation will come quickly.

My parents would meet halfway in Liberty, Indiana. I was so excited to see my family but so torn because I didn't want to leave my mom. I had such terrible anxiety for as long as I can remember. I'm sure it was because of the constant turmoil that was the only life that I knew. The recent changes had only made it worse. Nevertheless, off I went. No one had a choice; it was a court order. I remember the first time I saw my father after we left; it was the first visitation. He and his friend picked me up in a small sporty car. It was so hot that it kept overheating, and we had to turn the air conditioner off. I was so happy to see him but equally scared. I always had a buffer with my dad; Mom or Grandma would be around. This trip was just him, his friend, myself, and a whole lot of feelings. I had wondered what our home looked like. Would the bullet holes still be there? Would my bedroom look the same? Was he going to say bad things about Mom? Was he okay? I would worry about him. I hated how sad he must have been. I know that he had caused the whole thing, but he was still my father in the end. He was human and had feelings too.

On our way down, we stopped at the grocery store; we got Cocoa Puffs along with other things. He didn't have enough money to pay for the groceries, so we had to put things back. I felt embarrassed; this is the first time I realized how poor we were. Maybe it was a little time away, or possibly it was that Mom always shielded me from it. Then we went straight to Grandma's house. There were people there waiting for me. I remember the sound of the car tires on her gravel driveway. As soon as that car stopped, I flew out of it and straight to her arms. She hugged me and cried. It was in July, my birthday month. She had a birthday party for me. She had made a sign out of cardboard, and it was attached to the fence. There was cake, ice cream, and balloons.

We had so much fun. It was so comforting to be back at her house. I still remember what her house smelled like. It was very hot outside, and her house was very cool from the air conditioner. It smelled like the air conditioner, cigarette smoke, and Oil of Olay. It's amazing how you can remember a smell, and it takes you back to a place. It stirs up memories that are buried so deeply that you thought that they didn't exist anymore. I cherished that summer. Grandma had made a beautiful blue lace dress for me; she was a great seamstress. She would make me and my dolls matching outfits. There is a picture of me wearing it soon after I arrived. Grandma cooked for me and fed me anything I wanted and as much as I wanted. I'm talking Swiss cake rolls, Star Crunch, pork chops, and of course, all of the homemade cornbread and buttermilk I could handle. I ate Swiss cake rolls until I threw up one night. This is the summer I started eating my feelings. I was so torn, I knew the summer would not last forever, and I would have to leave my grandma again. I also really missed my mom and wanted to be with her. At the end of the summer, before

I went back home, my grandma and aunt Judy took me to get my pictures taken in the same dress. I had gained about twenty pounds. My father took me around to visit all of his friends; I felt like royalty. We would ride around in my father's black Silverado truck, listening to the radio, stopping off for a pop and candy bar at the Little Store. Everyone was so happy to see me. They all asked about what life was like in Indiana. I didn't really know how to act out what to say. Life was good there, but I knew it could hurt my grandma's and father's feelings if I said that.

I would kinda dance around the question; with all the confusion in my mind, I didn't even know how to articulate what I was feeling. So I just grabbed another Swiss cake roll. I just tried to tell people what they wanted to hear. Mom would tell me that this is my home now. We will never go back to live in Kentucky. My grandma would ask me if I wanted to come back to live there; everyone would ask me when I was coming back. I was very loved, and both sides of the family wanted me. I am grateful and blessed for this.

As they always do, summer came to an end; the last couple of days, I went around and said my goodbyes. It was bittersweet. I still to this day hate saying goodbye; I'd rather say, "See you soon," even if I know that's not true. Something inside of me just can't do it. I felt the heavy sadness from my grandma. She told me that when she found out that we left, she laid her head on the couch and cried for three days. This wrecked me; I was only eight years old. I knew it was going to crush her again, and there was nothing I could do about it.

When the day came to go back home to Indiana, we were soaked with tears; it got easier as we got on the road. Once we arrived in Liberty, Indiana, the halfway meeting place, my mom got off the car with a big smile, and I ran up and hugged her. Then it happened; she looked at me with such shock. She said, "You gained so much weight." She asked me what I ate; this was not the trip home I had imagined. I felt very ashamed and embarrassed. She said, "I don't even think your clothes are going to fit." Now in her defense, she always struggled with her weight, and she knew the pain that came with that. So now I had another awkward attribute to add to my list. I was now chubby with buckteeth, frizzy hair, and a Southern drawl.

It was time for me to decide if I was going to stay true to my Southern self with my Southern words and accent or try to fit into the mold of where I was planted. "XXX's and OOO's" by Trisha Yearwood was a favorite of mine. The part that says, "She's going to make it in her daddy's world. She's an American girl," always stuck with me. I was trying to figure out how to make it in both worlds.

Little did I know that this would be my last summer with my grandma.

When we pulled away from her house that day, things would never be the same. It's truly a blessing to not know what the future holds. I'm afraid it would have been unbearable at times.

Chapter 3

Our North Star Arrived on
a Honda Motorcycle

Hello, second grade. Here I am, Shake 'n Bake has arrived. I was in Mrs. Vanderhayden's class. I liked school as much as a cat likes a bath. Friends, I loathed school. None of it was my thing. I didn't like being away from home, schoolwork, or wondering who I would sit with at lunch. I felt very alone; dealing with all the emotions swirling around my head was clouding my thoughts. It was nearly impossible to concentrate. The schools in Kentucky were not as advanced as the ones in Indiana, so I was behind since *Jump Street*.

I have always had this superpower that is not at all in my control. If I am interested in a subject, I can rock it; it's nearly impossible to focus on it if I'm not. I don't love this about myself, but facts are facts. Math was not my friend; I didn't like it, nor did I understand it. So coming from a school that was behind academically, I had no chance of catching up on my own. My grammar and spelling were also subpar even though I always loved English class; I needed to do some catching up. So when things couldn't get any more awkward for me, it happened. The teacher wanted to put me in special education classes for math and English until I could catch up. I wanted to hide under a rock and never come out. I fought it tooth and nail, but in the end, it happened.

I can tell you this: I never thought I would be writing a book. I spent most of my life trying to overcome this poor self-image that imprinted on me. I am not smart enough; that's what it told me. Now in hindsight, I know that's not true, but that was my truth at the time. It haunted me and made me feel shame to my very core. I felt damaged, unworthy, and second-rate. I don't even think I told my husband about this until a few years ago. We have been married for eleven years. So let's add this up again: I'm the new kid, I have a Southern accent that you can cut with a butter knife, I have buck-teeth and frizzy hair, I stutter, I've gained about twenty pounds, and now I'm going into special education classes for math and English. Cool, this will be great for my self-esteem. Nevertheless, off I went.

When I would go to the special education room, it was like I was Wendy from *Peter Pan* about to walk the plank. Dread and embarrassment plagued me. The special education teachers turned out to be some of the kindest, most wonderful people that I have ever met. It was a gift to have known them; they made a huge impression on me. I was so emotionally damaged at this point in my life, and they were there to listen or to give me refuge during the day if I needed it. For them, I am grateful. I needed them more than I knew at the time.

The school year was in full swing at this point, and things at home were good. Every week I would talk to grandma and my dad. I was starting to adjust, and so was Mom. I had made some friends and was getting a new normal. Some of my weight started to come off, and I was slightly less awkward.

Then Mom got a call from Kentucky; Grandma was really sick and in the hospital. Off we went to see her; she had a blockage in her heart. What little bit of emotional stability I had was shaken. She was in the ICU, and I wasn't old enough to go in. I needed to be twelve; by God's grace, they let me in and didn't say anything. She was awake and aware, but she looked so pitiful lying in bed. I brushed her hair for her and just soaked in being in her presence. We stayed a couple of nights at the hospital, and then we had to go back to Indiana; Mom had to go back to work. We said our salty, tear-stained good-byes, and off we went. We drove the eight hours or so back home, and as we pulled into the driveway, my grandparents met us in the yard. They pulled Mom aside and were talking to her. Then Mom came over to me and told me that Grandma didn't make it. She had passed away on our way back home. I ran over to the pool area and sat in a chair and sobbed and sobbed and sobbed. I'm sobbing now as I write this. That was the very worst pain I had experienced.

A few days later was the funeral. I was a broken mess of emotions. Mom and I went back to Kentucky. We attended the funeral, said our last goodbye, then drove back to Indiana again. My poor mom worked seventy hours a week in a factory and emotionally struggled herself, then to see her child go through such pain and trauma. I can't imagine what she went through. Now, as a mother, I know that we feel our child's pain on top of our own.

God plucked us from the pit and brought us to a new place to start a new life. We had no idea of the things to come; that's how God works, though. He has such a great future for us that we couldn't even dream it up. He makes beauty from our mess.

I like to say that our North Star arrived on a motorcycle. Now my mom was 100 percent sure that she would never date or marry again. God said, "No, I have someone for you." She would see this nice man at work; his name is Chuck. They would talk and have lunch together from time to time. One day, Mom desired to put a note in his mailbox with her phone number on it. I have to give you all a side note here: this is in no way, shape, or form in my mom's character. I honestly thought she would never date again, let alone get married.

Chuck was in his backyard about a week before this and said a prayer; it went something like this: "God, I am so lonely, please give me somebody." This prayer was answered pretty quickly.

Now I had about all the change I could handle, so when I heard that my mom was going on a date, I was not happy about it. I was not even about to share my mom. She was the only consistent thing in my life. The date happened, and I thank God that it did. On their first date, they went out for Chinese food. Now there is a fifteen-year age difference between them. Mom asked, "How old did you say you were?" His response was, "How many kids did you say you have?" And just like that, they clicked. Our family thrives on teasing each other, sarcasm, and practical jokes. He was going to fit right in. Mom was really guarded for a long time; it took a very special person to have the patience and grace to wait for her heart to soften. That was Chuck. On their second date, he asked Mom if I would like to come along. That's when I think she knew this was meant to be. That meant a lot to me that he invited me along. I felt less worried about sharing with my mom. Chuck and I would butt heads now and then, but he was always good to me. He wasn't used to having a kid around, and I wasn't used to having a man around. After some time, we started to mesh. It was kinda nice to see Mom happy and not alone, even if I had to share her. So, friends, I cannot stay awake through a movie. Not unless it's a matinee; if it's past five, I will fall asleep. I can't sit still for that long and be conscious. All three of us went on another date; we decided to go to the movies. The newest Disney movie was *Pocahontas*. I really wanted to see it, and they let me pick. Sorry, Disney, it was not a favorite of mine or ours. It kinda sucked, and I fell asleep pretty soon after it started—give me a break, we had dinner first. A full belly and a late movie—I had no hope. So during my nap, I kept getting elbowed by Chuck to wake up, because if he had to watch *Pocahontas*, so did I. I deserved that—well played. Little did I know we were becoming a family.

Back at school, things were not much better. I would have a wave of emotion and just have to run out of class. I absolutely hate crying in front of people. I don't like showing emotion or people feeling sorry for me. I would wear Grandma's ring every day. It made me feel as though I had a part of her with me. I had developed this fear of my mom dying. I would get such terrible anxiety about it. I would make up excuses to call her from school. I had anxiety since I could remember, but now it was amplified. My mind was so full of anxiety and fears that I couldn't think straight to do my schoolwork. Somehow I just kept plugging along. Time passed, and summer vacation was approaching. I had to go down to Kentucky for visitation, and my safe place no longer existed. I was scared. I had my aunt Judy; I would stay at her house at night. She and Mom had it all planned out. At least there was a plan.

Summer vacation came quickly, and off I went—excited to see my dad and family and scared to death to face the reality that Grandma was gone. Being in another state helped me grieve, or at least help me avoid it. I wasn't around all the places that made me think of her. When I went back, it was so hard. I longed for the safe place that I had always known, but it was gone. I was now faced with the grieving process and had no clue how to get through it.

I would go with my dad in the daytime and stay with Aunt Judy at night. Dad had a new girlfriend; her name was Gina. She also had a daughter named Alicia. She was nothing like my mom but was living in our old house with my mom's belongings. I wasn't a fan of this at all. Her daughter had my old room. I knew how much my dad loved me, but I couldn't help but feel that we have been replaced. She was nice to me but liked to drink just as much as he did, and this was double trouble. They would have barn parties all of the time. I would get so upset because they would get drunk and just lose track of time and be up all night. I would just walk across the field to my aunt Judy's house. Her living there saved Mom and I more times than I can count.

Gina was a married woman; she was married to a man named Stevie. His family was wealthy. I believe they had oil on their property. She would leave Stevie with a pocket full of cash and run to my dad, live it up, and when the money ran dry, which it always did, she would go back to Stevie. As you can imagine, this caused a lot of strife in their lives and many fighting. This went on through the summer. Each day would be a roller coaster ride.

One day my dad and I went out for the day to go visiting; we went to one of his friend's houses deep in the "Holler." There was a scary Indian man that lived around there; he had a ton of vicious barking dogs. I was so scared of that house and the man, especially the dogs. We passed by his house on the way to our destination. I remember looking at the house and shuddering. We got to our destination point, and Dad had brought my go-cart. He got it out of the bed of the truck, and I rode it around the acres of rolling hills. It was a really fun day. Dad was drinking beer after beer after beer in the hot sun. The day was long, and I was hungry and wanted to go back to Aunt Judy's house. He said, "Just one more beer," and continue just one more beer until it was dark and very late into the night. I really wanted to call and check on my mom. He finally agrees that we can leave, but he said, "You have to drive." I didn't know how to drive; I was only nine years old at this time. Now I knew how to steer because I had been sitting on my dad's lap and steering ever since I could remember. This was a stick shift truck; I didn't know what to do. I was tired and scared and determined to go home. I said, "Okay, let's go." Sidenote: Who lets someone leave their house in that state, especially with a child with them? I'm not trying to be all judgy, but come on, people. So he loads my go-cart into the truck and closes the tailgate. He gets in the driver's seat and starts the truck. He said, "I'll do the shifter, and you have to steer the truck."

What is the actual heck! I am surprised that I agreed to that. He started to push the gas pedal, and I went to steering. We were winding our way through the washed-out gravel roads of the "Holler." We were getting close to the scary Indian's house. I could hear the dogs barking, and I'm not sure if I got nervous or if it was just the washed-out road, but I steered too close to the washed-out area, and it pulled us into the deep ditch. My dad tried to get the truck out of the ditch for some time, putting it into reverse and flooring the gas pedal. We were down too far to get out without help. I can't even believe what he did as I'm about to write this; he climbed out the truck window into the bed of the truck. He started my go-cart, dropped the tailgate, and drove off for help. I was left alone in the darkest of night. There were no streetlights or passing cars; there was only the Indian's house and the vicious barking dogs. It felt as if I sat there forever waiting for him to return. I knew there was nothing I could do to help myself. I was utterly alone, so I thought. I knew now Jesus was in that truck with me. I lay down and covered up with an old Marlboro towel and cried myself to sleep. I woke up to my dad talking to someone; one of his friends pulled us out of the ditch. We went home. He drove this time.

I went to Aunt Judy's house, and she asked where we were all night. I was supposed to stay the night at her house due to Mom's rule and agreed on it. I never showed up. I told her what had happened, and she warned me not to tell my mom, or she would never let me come back. I knew not to tell her to protect her. Things were fairly calm after that. Just usual life for a while until Gina and Dad got into a fight and left again. It was morning or at least early afternoon, and Dad had drank way too many beers. He was slurring his words and angry. He was telling me that he didn't like Chuck. I was scared and wanted to go to Aunt Judy's house and call my mom. He wasn't happy about that. I wanted him to quit drinking, and I hid his beer under the living room chair. He found it and drank it warm. Then he told me not to worry about calling Mom because she and Chuck were both dead. Chuck was a truck driver, and my Dad told me they drove off a cliff in his semi-truck. I still remember the panic that I felt run through my body. I felt the heat from the tips of my toes to the top of my head. I got hot and dizzy. A part of me believed him, and some part didn't. I sat there and cried, and he passed out. I ran out of the house and straight over to Aunt Judy's house. I was crying hysterically; she kept asking me what's wrong. I could barely breathe; I could hardly talk. I calmed down enough to tell her I needed to call Mom. I dialed her number, and she didn't answer. I called over and over again while the tears streamed from my eyes. My mom and Chuck were at work; they were both very much alive and well. Mom walked in the door during one of the phone calls; she answered, and I felt such relief. The rest of that summer break, I took refuge at Aunt Judy's house. I started to mentally and emotionally pull away from my dad. I'm not sure if it was just me getting older and realizing how dysfunctional our life was or realizing that I couldn't rely on him—maybe all of the above.

The alcohol and drugs had taken over. With having my mom and grandma as my safe places, I was very sheltered from him. I would be around him when he was fun; he would take me to get a candy bar or bring me a Happy Meal, or as we say in the South, a Happy Bucket; around certain holidays, they would put the Happy Meals in an actual bucket, and it could be decorated with stickers. The name stuck, and I called it a *happy bucket* for a long time. They would know when to keep me from him. I had a place where I could go to feel safe. Something I could count on. I thank God for Aunt Judy; without her, I would have felt even more lost. I was also blessed enough to have my cousin Nikki as well; she was four years older than me, but she was the closest thing to a sister that I ever knew.

Her house was so fun. My uncle, John, and aunt Debbie were so fun. They had a house full of older kids and all of their friends; it always seemed like a party at their house. I would go over and spend time with them. My aunt would make homemade ice cream and store it in the deep freezer in the garage. Nikki and I would sneak into it and hide and savor its creamy deliciousness. Nikki's grandpa lived way up the hill behind their house. We would often make the trek up the big hill to pay him a visit. You know the big vegetable drawers we have in our fridges? Well, he had one of those stocked full of candy bars. I'm not talking about fun-size either. They were full-size. It reminded me of a pirate treasure chest. They also had a big garden, and we would pull the green onions and eat them. A big black Doberman named Max would take shelter in the garage to find refuge from Southern summers' scorching rays. There was a little white church down the road, and Nikki and I would attend there on Sundays. I was clinging to anything that felt good and safe. I was trying to grieve and be okay at the same time—all the while being in a shaky environment.

I enjoyed the times I could with the people I could, all while such a storm of trauma, anxiety, fear, and instability plagued me. I hated nighttime; that's when my mind got still, and I would start to think. I was okay if I was busy. When the noise subsided, my eyes would fill with the sting of tears. I cried myself to sleep more times than I can even recall. It was sadly my nightly routine. It wasn't before long that the summer was over; I said my goodbyes, and I knew I would miss my Southern family very much. Little did I know that things were about to change once again.

Chapter 4

A Dark Dream

Have you ever had a dream that felt so real? So real that your emotions flutter around as if the dream had taken place in reality? That's the kind of dream I had. One night I went to bed as usual, and I had a dream that forever changed me. I was in a small canoe with my father. He was on one end, and I was on the other. The sky was black. The water was black. The space between us was black. The slow rock of the canoe slowly tossed side to side. I stared at him, and he stared at me. Then I asked him, "What did you do to mom?" He replied, "I'm going to be leaving soon." Once again, I repeated, "What did you do to Mom?" He replied, "I'm going to be going."

I was scared of him ever since that dream. Our relationship changed that night, and he didn't even know it. I couldn't make sense of it. When he would make the weekly phone call, I dreaded it; I would talk, but I had a deep internal knowledge of something very bad associated with him. After that day, things got easier. I didn't worry about him as much; there was a distance now.

Things kept getting more and more normal. I had started making more friends and adjusting to a new life, and enjoying my northern family. We were into a good routine. TGIF, come on, my '90s friends. Thank God it's Friday? Mom and I would pile up pillows and blankets on the floor along with a bunch of snacks and pop. We would celebrate the weekends. She was fun; I would usually have a friend over. It was so nice to have a group of friends.

Chuck was around more and more until he basically lived with us. He still had a home of his own where he had most of his stuff. His Dad built houses, and his mother decorated the homes. His dad grew up during the Great Depression and was very frugal. He had passed some homes to Chuck and his sister Barb. The home that Chuck still lived in had acres of sheds that housed all sorts of treasures. Tools, furniture, old glass bottles, knickknacks—you name it. It indeed was a treasure hunt. I wish I could have met them; they were salt-of-the-earth people I've been told. At this point, Chuck had four homes and a lake lot. He would take me with him to mow some of these properties on the weekend. I liked earning money. Then my friends and I would see who would take us to the mall.

It was a couple of weeks since my "dark dream." It was a school night. I had gone to sleep and woke up on my own. My mom always woke me up early for school. She had to be at work at 6:00 normally. She never slept in. This morning was different, so I thought; she slept in! I get to be late for school. I was so excited and giddy that I got to sleep in. I closed my eyes and drifted off to sleep again. Then I woke up a second time, and she still had not woken me up. I got worried that something was wrong with her. I get up and walk down the hallway from my bedroom to our living room. I see my mom, aunts, and uncles, and grandparents. They were all looking at me and crying. To their shock, I say, "Dad's dead, isn't he?" Their jaws dropped, and Mom hugged me crying and said, "Yeah, he's gone."

She explained that there was an accident; he had been shot, and he didn't make it. It turns out that Gina had come back another time, and she and my dad had gone to Renfro Valley in Mount Vernon, Kentucky. They had been running around that day, and Gina's husband Stevie and his brothers were looking for my dad. They knew Gina was with him, and they were all very angry. They stopped at my uncle John's house and asked where he was. Uncle John said that it was dark, and all he could see were headlights shining and someone asking if my dad was there. This was not a terribly odd thing because people would often be looking for beer or marijuana. He said, "I don't know where he is," which was the truth.

They left and went to the Exxon gas station in town. My dad and Gina were there. They had just gotten back in town. Stevie and his brother pulled my dad out of the car and shot him in the face; during the process, my dad had shot Stevie. They both fired shots and died. Gina was in the car and witnessed the whole thing. Her husband and her boyfriend are both gone, just like that. It was a double homicide. My cousin was inside the gas station. I'm sure he heard gunshots and went to see what had happened. He lay down on the ground with him so that he wouldn't be alone when he died. I thank him for this. I have never seen or heard from Gina. I can't wrap my head around what she went through. She had to tell her daughter that her dad was dead; she witnessed two shootings. Everyone in my family blamed her for this. While she was the reason the shootings happened, poor choices were made by all three people involved. If you ever read this, Gina, I forgive you. I no longer hold any resentment or anger toward you. I know you suffered, and I hope that you and your daughter can have healing and closure.

The crime scene must have been so heavy with grief; the shock of the innocent bystanders who saw this must have been plagued with emotions. The ripple effect that this caused is great. As the news spread through my loved ones from one phone call to another, the pain increased and became more real. My dear uncle John struggled with this with such a heavy heart. He later shared with me that he felt that he should have stopped Stevie when he came to his house looking for my dad. He said that he didn't realize it was him and that all he could see were headlights. I did all I could do to reassure him that none of this was his fault, and there was no way he would have been able to know what was about to happen.

The funeral service was shortly after, and Mom and I made the trip back to Kentucky.

I was numb. I'm sure Mom was too. Nevertheless, off we went. It was great to see my family when we arrived, but everyone was so broken, as I was. We went to the Little Store that Dad and I would frequent. Nolan, the store owner, was there and obviously knew me well. He loved our family, and for support, he had a container for people to donate money to cover funeral costs. It had a picture of Dad and me under a tree; this picture was taken last summer I saw him. We were at his best friend's house. I remember it like it was yesterday.

When I saw our picture, it opened a floodgate of emotions. Everyone I love is dying. This is such an awful, ugly thing that happened. Everyone's talking about the shooting. I will always be the poor girl that everyone feels sorry for. I'll never be able to go through a day without crying. I'll always be sad. Nothing is ever gonna be okay or stay the same. Then I told myself, *Don't cry while you're standing here.* Crying in front of people is hard for me; it's uncomfortable, and I hate it. I breathed through it and, just like a switch, I turned it off. I couldn't deal with any more heartache. I was shutting down.

At the funeral, there were a lot of people there. I sat with my mom, and I was near my aunt Judy and uncle John. Their sad broken faces killed me; my pain was so great, and being so immersed in the pain of those I loved was unbearable. I was a ten-year-old girl when this happened. The funeral was open casket; he had been shot in the face, and it had to be reconstructed. I don't think I looked very hard at his face. It was too much. I did stand there and hold his hand. When everyone was ready to leave and close the casket, I walked back to watch it; my aunt Judy pulled me away, but I pulled back. I needed to see it close; I knew that was the last time I would ever see him again. Seeing it close gave me closure. We all threw roses onto the casket at the grave site as the dirt was filling the hole. I remember the dirt falling onto the roses as they were eventually lost in the earth.

My mind was swirling with gracious people telling me how much he loved me and how sorry they were. I never really knew what to say. Through all of this tragedy, I always knew I was loved. What I didn't know was how to move forward. How to go back to school and tell all the kids who asked where I had been or why I was so sad. I would put on a happy face to avoid showing my emotions at school or what I dreaded the most—crying in front of people. When anyone would start to ask questions, I could feel the burning and sting of hot tears brewing in my eyes. I would avoid it and try my very best to appear normal. As for normal, I mean a regular Indiana girl with no accent and one with a normal family. A normal girl whose dad wasn't murdered and a normal girl who didn't have horrible anxiety and didn't worry about her mom dying every day. That kind of normal. I asked what was going on inside and said my dad died of a heart attack, and I began to try to mold myself into someone else.

I didn't know who that would be; what I did know was that I couldn't be the same as I was now. My mom kept trying to talk me into getting counseling, and I said, "Nope, I'm fine." I honestly believed that I was fine. Our brains are so overwhelmingly complex. The pain and trauma was so much that my brain tucked them deeply away so it wouldn't be at the top of my mind. I honestly thought that I was okay. I believed it.

If I had a time machine, I would have returned to the ten-year-old me and told her: Alicia, you are strong, *worthy*. The world needs your story; share it and help those around you who may have a similar struggle. Don't shrink back or cower because your story is different from other people's stories. Yours is riddled with sadness and trauma but adorned with so much love and happy times. It's a mixed bag, but it's your bag. Your family loved you not perfectly but fiercely. Your dad was a broken man; he loved you but made poor choices. He had his heavy bag of issues that he never sorted through and was drowning himself in alcohol and drugs so that he can escape from something. Maybe it was the death of his dad at a young age. He lost his role model; he didn't have a man to show him how to be a man or to speak some sense into him when he needed it. He didn't choose that over you; he was just trying to survive himself. He was your dad, and you loved him well. Remember the good times you had with him—all of the long rides in his pickup truck blaring country music so loud that you couldn't hear anything else. Or when he would take you and a friend "T-topping." (He would borrow a friend's car that had a T-top; he would take the top off and let us stand up while he was cruising the countryside. He would be zigging and zagging through the mountains blaring music and having the time of our life. He would make this weird duck face to make me laugh when I was upset. He would let me sit on his lap as we would mow the yard. He would tell me that someday he was going to make it a big theme park with all sorts of rides and call it Nuker Duker Land; that was one of my nicknames as a kid.)

Your grandma loved you more than you know, and she knew how much you loved her. She was a safe refuge for you and your mom. She loved you both well. She also had many of her battles. She carried so much grief that her husband died; she carried the pain of her children losing their father. She never recovered from that loss. She had a hard time disciplining your dad when he needed it because she felt sorry for him losing his dad. Then he got older and more out of control, and then there was nothing that she could do. His anger was out of control, and it was out of her hands. She carried sadness and worry. She could have laid that down and fought for healing, but maybe she didn't know-how. Carry her memory close to you as you always will. Remember the way she smelled like Oil of Olay and loved you like crazy. When you're sad, think of her little kitchen with the green fridge and the strawberry decorations that you would look at as she would make you a milkshake with her hand blender. Or when she would make a Jack's Pizza, and you two would sit at the counter and drink RC Cola and have a moon pie for dessert. Remember her always-full cup of coffee and her smoking cigarette in a full ashtray. That Caboodles full of lipstick, in every shade of red, that you could fathom. Remember how you felt when you were around her, how you knew that you were safe and were loved above all else, even herself. Tuck that was feeling in a safe place and pull it out when you need comforting.

Remember that you are a Southern girl with a pretty awesome accent. I promise you, my ten-year-old self. When you are thirty-four, you will wish you still had it. But also know that you are just as much a northern girl as you are a Southern girl. You will make it in both worlds. You won't always be chubby with buckteeth. Don't forget the way the creek sounded during the stillness of the day. Don't forget the way the bullfrogs sound at night—they were so loud—or the kindness and hospitality of the Southern people. They love hard, feed you well, and you never feel like an outsider. That is also instilled in you. You left there, but it can never be taken from you.

Remember where you came from, learn from the bad lessons that you saw lived out around you. Don't be consumed by it, though. When hard things happen, take time to process them, and then you can move on. Don't cover it up and let it fester in the dark. Shine the light on it, and it won't seem as scary. Girl you will be okay. You will be more than okay; you will use what you have been through to help women like your grandma, who was stuck in grief and worry. It will help women like your mom that have struggled with abuse and pain. You have been given this mountain to show other women that it can be moved. Your story will not be in vain. You will be restored. One woman's success shows others around her that whatever it is can be done. Don't lose who you are because that's where the magic is scars and all.

One last thing, my ten-year-old self. Your heart is very soft and kind. The world will say you need to toughen up and not be so sensitive. Don't listen, that is what makes you so sensitive to other people's needs. You have a gift; you can find the one person in the room who is choking back tears but is wearing a big smile. You can see through that; that is your gift. You can find those hurting people and love them. You can share your story with them; they will see that you know pain, loss, and heartache and see you're still here. Not only are you here, but you are as strong as you are soft and kind. You are a fighter, and you never quit; you have been knocked down more times than you can count, and you keep getting up. If you can do it, so can they. You will show them, lead them, and love them.

Chapter 5

A New Normal

Will things ever go back to normal? No, they will not. The normal that you once knew is never to return again. How could things ever be the same? How could I ever be the same? How could I ever be okay again?

This was my reality. Broken, scarred, and lost. I was not scared for my safety and not lost as I didn't know where I was. I didn't know who I was; I was scared because everything I knew was different. My old comforts were gone; where do I begin? My poor mom was working through the trauma of her childhood and working seventy-plus hours a week. Chuck was around most of the time, and I had never known a man quite like him. I just knew something would happen in the back of my mind: he would get mad and hit my mom, or maybe he would start drinking and get violent.

Have I mentioned what kind of guy Chuck was and is? He is gentle and kind. He doesn't smoke, do drugs, or even drink—other than maybe a nice cold Icehouse once a summer, if that. He works hard and rarely yells. To this day, I've heard him yell as many times as I can count on my fingers. But I was waiting for the other shoe to drop. Things won't stay stable and safe for long. I wanted to prepare myself for when things got bad again. It wouldn't hurt me if I didn't get close to him when he left or got mean. If no one really knows me and gets close to me, then I'll be safe.

I'd say it's safe to say that we all bonded over meals. Particularly over buffet dinners at Food Lin restaurant. There was a mavericks bookstore a few stores down in the strip mall. I would usually get to pick out a magazine such as teen *Bop* or *Tiger Beat*. I loved the posters that come inside those magazines. Devon Sawa and JTT; for those of you who may have lived under a rock, that's Jonathon Taylor Thomas. They were pretty rad, if I may say so myself. Now I was not allowed to tape or use thumbtacks to put my posters on my walls. So I got a little inventive, and I got some string and taped the string to the poster, then taped the other end of the string to my ceiling! I was never told not to tape or pin anything to my ceiling. There's always a loophole, right? When Mom came into my room, she was surprised but had to laugh. The dangling posters stayed where I stuck them. I also loved *Teen Vogue*. In all my awkward glory, I would see these beautiful women and wanted to be like them—makeup how-tos and hair tricks and tips. I became enamored with the beauty business. As I write this book, I am in my eleventh year as a cosmetologist. I recently opened a small salon and talked my mom into quitting her job and becoming a nail tech. She now has her own independent business inside my salon, which I love so much. I also have two friends that work in my salon. I have been so blessed to create a happy, creative space where we can all work and prosper.

So in my attempt to feel better in my skin, I began to experiment with hair color. I could write a separate book solely about all of the awful things I have done to my hair and my friends' hair. Girls, if you are reading this, I'm sorry. You know who you are.

It all started with highlights; my mom did my very first set of high lights in our kitchen. They were the kind you painted on; nowadays, we call that balayage. It went great, crisis averted. Until there was some leftover, I mixed it up the next day and made my bangs blonder. Then I wanted more and more blond. So we went to the highlighting cap, the kind where you put the plastic cap on and pull the hair through with a little hook. Then slather the bleach over the cap. Cover and let it cook. Doesn't that sound fancy? This is all good until the roots grow out, then we would repeat the process until my hair would be white. The only logical thing to do was get a box of brown hair color and go back to my natural color, ha! There are a lot of things that can go wrong with this. I grabbed an ash brown. It made my whole head grayish-green. I panicked and called my grandma to give me a ride to the store to get a highlighting kit to fix it. So in my panicked fury, I mistakenly ripped the holes too big in the cap. As the color was processing, I kept checking it, and I noticed my scalp burning; the bleach had bled through the ripped holes. I ripped the cap off and rinsed my hair. You guys, my hair was grayish-green with orange cheetah spots. Many tears were shed over this one. It was even close to Halloween; what the heck. I didn't even need a wig if I wanted to go trick-or-treating. My mom came home from work to find me looking like a crazy hot mess express and crying. I informed her that I would not be going to school the next day or any day until this crisis was over. Once again, we go back to the store and get another box of dye. This one was okay, and life went on. Until next time.

Sometime after that, my best friend told me that she knew how to layer hair. "I know how to layer hair. I saw someone do it on TV. You just pick up some pieces and make them shorter." "Okay," I said. "then I'll do yours." So I am the first to get my haircut; my hair looked chopped up to my horror. Needless to say, my dear friend didn't want to take her turn in the styling chair.

This ushered in the era of the infamous "golden mushroom"; Chuck coined this phrase. That poor guy had to run my friends and I down to the drugstore late at night many times so we could run inside and try to find a solution for whatever mistake that just happened on our head.

So guess what I did? I chopped it off to my chin—by myself, just like that. That was brave, right? It was all one length, and they didn't have flat irons back then—wow, I just really aged myself. So I would take a curling iron and smooth it and tuck in under a bit. With my botched golden blond and my mushroom cut, I really was a looker. My friend, you know the one who we liked to ruin each other's hair? She wanted a mushroom cut too! So, I did it. You won't even be able to wrap your head around this one; her mom wanted the haircut too. So I did it again. What is the actual heck? A smart adult woman (whom I adore) let me touch her hair with scissors.

There it was. I had found my passion. I loved to make women feel good about themselves. Thankfully my skills improved over the years.

Life was starting to fall into what would be my new normal. New routines and staying busy kept my mind from going in the wrong direction. I stayed very busy with friends and with Mom and Chuck. My mom was always so good about letting me have friends over and doing fun things. We would make these fajita kits and bake brownies. I was not allowed to go many places, so our house was the hangout spot. Mom was super protective over me. It drove me crazy at the time, but now I understand it completely. I do the same with my son. If he gets away with anything, it will be a miracle.

I had started to tell myself I'm fine. "You're over everything, and you're okay." Inside I was hoping and praying that no one would ask where my dad lived or if my parents were together. The wave of emotions would hit me like a ton of bricks, and I would feel the tears welling up in my eyes. When this would happen, I would simply say, "He died of a heart attack." Then it would be followed by, "I'm so sorry." I never knew what to say to that. I knew that people meant well, and they really were sorry. I would say, "It's okay," even though it wasn't. What had happened was anything but okay.

Time was my friend; the more time that went on, the better things got better. I got closer to Chuck, and it was nice to have a more normal family life. Mom was happy, and that made things easier for me. Time was moving on, and I was getting a little older.

One day Chuck came to me and said, "I would like to marry your mom and adopt you. I would like to be your dad. We can be a family." God is indeed in the restoration business. He was restoring what was lost. I never once thought that I would get another dad. I said yes and was excited but wondered what people would think if I changed my last name. He wanted to adopt me at fifteen. What an amazing man. Chuck always had the utmost respect for my uncle John. He asked him if it would be okay with him if he adopted me. Uncle John said yes; he didn't like the idea of me changing my last name from *Hollin*, but he was aware that it would change if I got married anyway, so he gave his blessing. We went to the courthouse and did all the paperwork. Mom and now *my* dad also got married at the courthouse.

Chuck has the kindest family I had ever met. They are so kind that it didn't even seem real. His parents had already passed away, but he had a sister named Barb, a brother-in-law named Wayne, and two nieces named Julie and Laurie. They were all so generous, soft-spoken, and calm. Much different from what we were used to. Aunt Barb would invite us over for dinner about once a month; she would make baked chicken and strawberry shortcake. Her chicken was so delicious. She would look at me and genuinely listen and want to hear what I had to say. She makes you feel important. She was never too busy for you or distracted. Just like that, we got a whole new extended family. My cousins Julie and Laurie are two of my dear friends. We would have Christmas dinners together, and whatever I was doing, they would support me wholeheartedly. Julie was always so cool. She had a very natural beauty and style. She always had a natural coolness to her; she shopped at the coolest stores. I tried to mold myself after her style. If Julie had silver hoop earrings, then I wanted silver hoop earrings too. I imagine that what it may be like having a cool older sister. Laurie, she is a natural cheerleader. If you have a creative bone in your body, she will find it; she will support you and help you make a game plan on how to succeed. She is still one of my biggest cheerleaders, and her love and support are some of the reasons I am where I am today.

Chuck also meshed well with our side of the family. They were much louder and crazier. We often have food fights and argue. It's kinda like a *My Big Fat Greek Wedding* family, but we're not Greek. We tease and wrestle and live to embarrass each other. One of my very favorite food fight stories was at a birthday party in the summer at my grandparents' house. This took place a couple of years ago. My uncle Scott smashed a piece of cake in my face. This was not an unusual event. So naturally, I returned that favor. Then it turned into an all-out crazy food fight. When things calmed down, he went over to the water hose and started to clean himself off. Then I kept dumping stuff on him and didn't let him realize what I was doing. So we would stand up and think he had gotten all the food off, and there would still be frosting on him. After this went on for a while, he got mad and went over to the swimming pool and jumped in, in only his underwear. While he was rinsing off, one of the younger kids threw his clothes in the pool. So he wrapped a towel around him; he was steaming mad and trying not to lose his cool. Then my mom was videotaping this whole thing, and then my other uncle Jeff ripped off the towel, so he's standing in his underwear in front of our whole family. His blue underwear had turned purple from a laundry mishap. This did not make things any better for him. Then the video made its way to Uncle Scott's work friends; he could thank his brother for that. He still hears about that to this day. I could go on and on about all of the pranks and food fights we have had with our family. Teasing and embarrassing, and smashing food is our love language. Weird, but it's ours. My uncle Jeff and I have the same teasing relationship; when I was young, he would get ready to go on dates. I swear he would put on a bottle of cologne. I would call him shunk, and he would call me weasel. Both of my uncles are like big brothers. See, as an only child, God provided me with all the people that I need in my life. He will do the same for you too.

Do you all remember the nickname I used to have? Corn Bread? My uncles wanted to get that as my license plate when I got my first car. My mom said no. Thanks, Mom; good call on that one.

Now I had a normal family life with a mom and a dad: a dad that was a father, and a darn good one at that. Our home was stable; he loved my mom and only built her up and would never harm her. This man did more for me than I could ever express. I feel from the bottom of my heart that God used him to save us. He's seventy-two years old now; Mom and Dad are still together and going strong. Because of him, I had guidance and security, and our son Jackson has a grandpa. He calls him *Poppy*. As we drove away from our home in Kentucky, we were so blessed we were leaving our old life, and God had already had the puzzle pieces aligned for our new life to unfold. He makes beauty out of our mess; He sure did that for us.

Chapter 6

Diet Drama and Living on My Own, Kinda

Let's talk diets, shall we? So at this point in my life, I had been on more diets and eating plans than I can even count, but let's try. I have done Atkins, vegan, no grains, no oils or fats, counted calories, counted carbs, counted macros. I've also done the HCG diet, where you give yourself shots in your stomach and eat small amounts of food. I've eaten only five hundred calories a day and excessively worked out. I've done Herbalife, I've done juice cleanses, I've taken diet pills, and I've fasted. This sounds so crazy because it really is. I have never had a healthy relationship with food. I am an emotional eater, and I learned this from a young age: when I'm happy, I will eat; when I'm sad, I eat; when I'm stressed, I eat. Food has always been my comfort.

My friend's really cool older sister would eat what she wanted then purge. This sounded like a great idea. If I couldn't control what I ate, I could just "get rid of it." I tried this, and it worked. I found something that worked—or so I thought, so I would eat five hundred calories a day and jog for an hour every day. Then if I just couldn't take it and wanted to eat whatever I wanted, I would. Then I would make myself throw up and be back to normal with no harm done. I dropped weight fast. I went from a size 10/12 to a 4/6 in a couple of months. I felt amazing. My confidence was through the roof, and thankfully my bad haircut had grown out. Cute boys were starting to pay attention to me, and I was getting so much attention. "Alicia looks so good. Wow, how did you do that?" I certainly wasn't going to share my dirty little secret with anyone. For the first time in my life, I felt in control and confident. I had arrived, so I thought. I started to get more popular at school, and my self-doubt was a thing of the past. I love to shop, and I got to get cool trendy clothes, and I looked great in them. All I had to do was keep starving myself, excessive exercise, and purge if I ate too much. Sounds realistic, right?

It all came to a head when I was seventeen years old, and I had just started driving. I took my cat to the vet's office close to our house in the little town of Edwardsburg, Michigan. I was holding her at the office window, and my eyesight started to get dark, and I felt weird. I turned away to walk over to the sitting area to have a seat, and then I passed out. The cat shredded me. I woke up on the floor with people standing over me. I had peed my pants and was mortified. My blood sugar had dropped, and then I also dropped. Now, what do I do? I had to stay thin, but I couldn't go around passing out and peeing my pants. This was not a good trade-off. I had some extra pants in my car; a nice lady in the office went out and got them for me. I drank some sugar water, changed my pants, and drove home. I had huge claw marks on my arms that were dripping blood. What was I going to tell my parents?

I got home, and they saw the claw marks on my arms right away, and they asked what had happened. I told them the story, all the while leaving out that I peed my pants. My mom said, "You're starving yourself, and you need to eat." Dad went to Taco Bell and got me a bean burrito. That was always my weakness; I could eat Taco Bell anytime and anywhere. I was now afraid that I was going to pass out while driving and get in a wreck or pass out and pee my pants at school. I was at a loss for what to do. I felt confused about how to maintain this thin weight. So I started a series of weight-loss plans and yo-yo diets. I would try to limit my "bad foods"; anything that was not meat, fruit, or veggie was a "bad food." I no longer called any food group bad—some are better than others, and some food is just crap, but as soon as I start to restrict myself from any food or type of food, I just start to crave it. Eventually, I'll cave in and overeat. Then I would say, "I'll just start again tomorrow." Sidenote: You don't need a new day to start fresh. Take a deep breath and start again right where you are. Every moment is a chance to start fresh. Just as you may have had a poor choice of food doesn't give you a free-for-all until the next day. This is a terrible cycle that was very easy for me to get stuck in.

Would you please avoid this at all costs? So from this point on, my skinny jeans were a struggle. I obsessed over my weight to the point that it consumed me. I had lost a lot of joy, and fun things passed as I was busy working out excessively. I heard a lot of "You're skinny, you need to eat." Well, if I ate, I wouldn't stay skinny. Or so I thought. Eating the right foods and a healthy amount of exercise to maintain a healthy heart and body were key. Unfortunately, I didn't know exactly how to go about that at the time. Food portions were also a big issue. A serving of meat or protein in roughly the size of your palm, and a serving of cheese the size of a matchbox. I went from eating basically nothing to eating mostly what I wanted, and the weight came back fast. I would resist buying bigger pants, so I would get jeans that had a lot of stretch or brands that ran bigger. I would think, *Okay, next week, I'll really crack down and get this weight off.*

I ventured out on my own at the young age of seventeen—well, sorta on my own. My parents had a small rental house on County Road 15 in Elkhart, Indiana, and they let me live there. My dad's dad built it for his mother-in-law some time back. It was either build her a home, or she was moving in with them. He started building. It was a very small—about six hundred square feet—adorable cottage house.

It was very old but had a lot of character and was adorable to me, and it was mine! I had a garage that ended up staying filled with boxes of all of my junk, but hey, it's a garage. There was one bedroom and one bathroom, a living room with a fireplace, and a kitchen. It was like a dream come true. I had total freedom. I could come and go as I please, and that was almost unbelievable. I had a tiny fridge that was stocked with almost nothing besides spray butter and Diet Pepsi, and the pantry held cans of tuna, peas, and instant white rice. I lived off of this. My mom had given me a beautiful set of dishes that were in raspberry color. It came with the mixing bowls and a teapot. She had this vintage bookcase that was in Dad's family, and we put it next to the stove and displayed the mixing bowls and assorted pretty things. My parents had also purchased a pub-style bistro table with two chairs for my sweet little kitchen. I still have them in the storage room in our house. I can't stand to part with it. Maybe someday Jackson will want it for his first dorm or apartment. Hold back the tears, Alicia. The living room had a leather couch that was so broken down that you may as well have sat on the floor. The bedroom was so tiny that it held my full-size bed, and when I went to vacuum, there was just enough room from the bed to the wall—one pass, and I was done.

The bathroom had a miniature bathtub and a hobbit-sized sink. Dad pulled those out and replaced them with a shower stall and regular-height sink. I also had a closet area in the room that joined the bathroom. It had previously been a second bedroom, but that wall was taken down to make a larger bathroom some time back. That became a walk-in closet.

The first night alone, my mom was over helping me move stuff in; I started to get scared and didn't want her to leave. Of course, my seventeen-year-old self was too cool to admit it. She said goodbye and left. I went into my little cottage and had every light on in the whole house. I sat down on my broken couch and thought to myself; *This is what it's like to be an adult.* I couldn't wait to wake up in the morning and have coffee.

So what could make this whole situation any better? If my best friend came to live with me? Yes, you guessed it. My best friend, Heather, was over all the time; and we just decided, why don't you move in? I asked my parents, and they said yes; her mom agreed, and then it was settled. I would get a roommate. I was working at Prime Table in Niles, Michigan; I was a waitress at the time. I was the worst waitress ever; people with ADD cannot remember what ten people want at any given time. "Can I have silverware?" "I want some ketchup." "Can I get a napkin?" Come on people gave me a break. They were so needy. Nevertheless, somehow, they didn't fire me.

Heather had the day off and was ready to move in; she was a vet tech in Mishawaka, Indiana. I had not made an extra key yet, but a living room window was unlatched; that was slightly smaller and up high, but the couch was under it. There was a ladder in the garage. I told her to get the ladder out, climb in the window, and land on the couch. Now the family that lived in my little cottage had moved next door; my dad's sister Barb had inherited that house. Their names were Dean and Renee. They had only moved out a couple of months before. So Heather gets the ladder out and brings it over to the window, and climbs in; just as she has one leg in and she's straddling the window, a police officer pulls in the driveway. Can you believe this? She looks like a burglar. So she gets half of her body—which is in the house—out and climbs down the ladder. The officer is very skeptical of her and asks her what she's doing; she explains that she's moving in and tells him that I didn't have a key made yet. He asks to see her driver's license; I don't think he was buying it. Dean, the next-door neighbor that had recently moved out of the cottage to my aunt's house next door, comes over to save the day. He tells the officer that he knows who she is and that she's moving in. So the officer asks who he is and wants to see his identification. Dean had not changed his address yet, and it still matched the cottage house address. You guys, can you believe this? The police officer was like, "Sir, why does it say that you live here?" This was almost unbelievable; I'm laughing even as I'm writing this. This story will never get old. He explained the situation, and all was well.

He ended up leaving and not taking her to jail. She proceeded to move in; when I got home from work that night, it was the coolest thing ever. I came home to my little cottage, and my best friend was there for a continual sleepover. We shared our stuff and would go out to Steak 'n Shake all the time for coffee. We were real grown-ups at the ripe old age of seventeen. She was almost eighteen; I'm the younger one by a month and a day. I always remind her of that.

So all was well in our little world; we would have our friends over. Since most of our friends were mutual, it was easy. We had a fire pit in the backyard and would have bonfires and drink cheap beer. I'm pretty sure there are still beer cans embedded in the earth around that firepit. Our meals consisted of canned tuna and rice with peas and spray butter. Thankfully she also shared a love of strange food combinations. It made grocery shopping very simple.

A couple of months after moving into the cottage, we both graduated from Edwardsburg High School. I had also started dating my very first real boyfriend. Now I really thought that I was grown up. Just a short time after graduation, I started taking classes at Ivy Tech College. My dream and calling was to be a hairstylist. I had some well-meaning people in my life that told me I would never make any money in that industry and that I needed to get into the medical field. So I looked into being a nurse, and the amount of schooling needed was way more than what I wanted to commit to. I wanted to finish school and get on with life as soon as possible. So I signed up for classes to be a surgical technician. It required fewer classes, and I knew I could go back to school later to continue my schooling if I wanted to. My dear dad paid for my classes—how lucky was I? I was honestly so tired of school and just wanted to have fun. I was not in the mindset to go to college at that time. I told my parents that, and they said that I might never go if I waited. I understand where they're coming from. I was so immature and irresponsible. It was so exciting having a real boyfriend; I quickly became consumed with him and his life and didn't pay much mind to my own life or goals. I started being with my friends less and less, and school was certainly not my main focus. My boyfriend was not in college and worked for his dad; it was a day shift job. I also worked during the day and attended school at night. He would want to go to dinner, movies, and parties, and I was easily swayed. I started to miss school here and there, and it didn't seem to be a big deal.

Attending college classes was very different from high school because they didn't care if you didn't turn in your work. They just gave you a big fat zero. They didn't chase you down or call your parents or even ask you about it. *So* a few assignments slipped, then a few more. Now, I am over my head in past assignments that I don't even know how to catch up. So what does an immature now eighteen year old do? They quit going to school! Why I thought that this was my only option, I have no clue. I didn't even tell my parents. My dad would ask me about my grades, and I would say, "I don't know, I haven't gotten anything back," which was not a lie; I hadn't gotten anything back because I hadn't turned anything in. After a while, he just called the school, and they informed him that I hadn't been there in quite some time. He was so disappointed, so was my mom. I wasted his hard-earned money, and I was dishonest; I felt horrible. Of course, they forgave me, but I knew the disappointment would need time to fade.

I continued working as a waitress, and I liked the quick cash. I would usually work at breakfast restaurants because I liked the hours. Having my nights free was great; I'm still the same way. There's something so refreshing about getting up early, getting your work done, then having the rest of your day as your own. If there were a weekend that my job would want time to work, I would just call off or quit and get another waitress job next week. As I'm writing this, I cannot believe that it was me! I want to shake that silly girl and talk some sense into her. My work ethic sucked, but I had fun, and now I have some good stories to tell. There's always a silver lining, right?

I had very little freedom as I grew up, and I went a little crazy for a summer; I had my friends and my freedom. I barely had two nickels to rub together, and I didn't mind a bit. What I'm about to say would make my dear role model Dave Ramsey shudder. Love you, Dave. I would spend every single dollar I had. Abercrombie and Fitch were super-popular at the time, and if I had twenty-five dollars, I would rush to the mall and get a graphic tee shirt. I wouldn't even care if I had grocery money. I knew I could always go to my parents' house and eat.

My boyfriend—let's call him Adam. Adam was a couple of years older than I, and he had gotten an ID from one of his friends. She was a little older than I. We looked nothing alike at all. I had curly blond hair, and she had long brown hair and were about a foot taller than I. He wanted me to go to bars with him; I was so scared to use this thing. I never got in trouble, and the thought of getting in trouble for fraud was enough to send me into a panic. Well, he talked me into using it; the first place was at Hacienda. We sat in the bar area, and I ordered a margarita. It actually worked! Were these people blind? The next place I used it was the Sports Page in Granger, Indiana. They're closed now, so I think it's okay that I'm writing this, and no, they didn't close down for serving minors. This was a small-town bar that was a lot of fun. They would have bands often and had a pretty good DJ most of the time. The dance floor was usually full, and every Thursday was penny pitcher night. It was a five-dollar cover, and you are good to go. Now that I think back on it, I'm sure they knew it wasn't me, at least some of the time, but since it was a real ID, they were covered, and I don't think that they cared. I would always have a racing heartbeat every time I was about to hand the ID over, and each time, I got to breathe a sigh of relief.

I started to spend a lot of time at Adam's house, and I saw Heather less and less; she worked a day job during the week and would work at Club Landing on weekends at night. She started hanging out with a different group of people, and so did I. Eventually, we were like ships passing in the night. After a while, she moved out, and I moved in with Adam. This was a very sore subject with my family. Living together with a man before being married was very frowned upon. My mom was a bit more understanding, but my dad wants nothing to do with it. He came to our apartment one time in the three years that Adam and I were together. Don't worry, Heather and I are still friends seventeen years later. We spoke on the phone yesterday. Ever since I was a little girl, all I ever wanted was to be a wife, have lots of babies, decorate a home, and do all things domestic, and do hair, of course. At first, the apartment life was great, nice and new, and comfortable. It was a corner apartment, and there was a sliding glass door with a small patio area where we could grill. I would grocery shop and cook dinners—thank You, Jesus, that my cooking got better. We had a washer and dryer in the kitchen. We also had a dishwasher; this was dreamy. There was always a bit of shame wrapped in this new part of my life. I knew it was wrong to be living the way I was. I knew that I was letting my parents down, letting myself down, and letting God down. I knew that I was made for more, yet I kept walking down the same path, entwined with guilt and disappointment.

Chapter 7

Why Buy the Cow If You Get the Milk for Free?

You have all heard this saying, right? Why buy the cow if you get the milk for free? Sis, it's true. I didn't believe it at the time either, but hindsight is twenty-twenty. It sounds like an old-fashioned saying for old people who just don't understand how the world is now. That's what I thought. I can tell you from experience that this did not work for me.

So I have my first real boyfriend at the age of eighteen; I was a very independent kind of gal who loved being around her friends, working out, having fun at the mall. I knew my worth, and I didn't need a boyfriend. I loved my alone time; being an Enneagram 3 and and having introverted tendencies, I need it. I felt bad for the girls that were always chasing down a guy and getting their heartbroken.

I would think to myself, *That poor thing, she doesn't know her worth.* Sadly, I quickly fell into the same trap. Let me tell you the story.

Adam was a very persuasive fun type of guy. He was a little rough around the edges and a bit of a hothead. Why do we like those bad boys? I had no clue of how easily I was persuaded until I was right in the thick of it, and it was a total mind-bender. Now we are living in our apartment, and I am cooking, cleaning, working, and partying way more than I should. We would be out late and have friends over all the time. I was burning the candle at both ends. I wasn't taking care of myself. I quickly fell away from my friends and was mainly only with Adam and his friends. I didn't see my family as much, and my old habits—you know, the ones that involved self-care and alone time?—were a thing of the past. I was spiraling out of control, and all I knew was that I loved Adam, and if I wanted to be with him, I had to be in his world. My friends would invite me out, and the response would always be, "I'm sorry I can't" or "I'll see if Adam can come." After some time, they stopped asking as much, and we all grew apart.

The Alicia that I once was is now slipping away. I did not like who I was becoming. I was dependent on his approval and love. My life revolved around him. He would go out and party with his friends. I was so insecure that he would cheat on me, and he inevitably did, which crushed me. There was a person that I went to school with since the first grade—let's call her Mary. She had dated him for a couple of years before I had started dating him. She was still in love with him and tormented me for being with him. There are so many stories about this series of unfortunate events. I'll give you a heads-up, though: God worked this for my good. Even though I was off my path and a hot mess, He still had me; He is not a fair-weather God. He is a kind God; He's not vengeful. He loves us.

When she found out that I was dating him, she called me and told me that she didn't like it and that I shouldn't see him anymore. I told her, "I'm sorry you're upset, but I like him, and I'm going to date him." Bless my sweet baby heart; I should have listened to Mary. These were not my people; I did not belong. This led her to prank-call me at multiple hours of the day and night. She would have her friends do it, too; some of them were even my old friends, which was super-hurtful. Then Adam started to see her behind my back; he was not known to be a one-woman kind of guy—hello, red flag. She would go down the street and wait for me to leave, and she would pull in and hang out while I was at work. Then they kissed, and her friend, that is our mutual friend called and told my dad. So humiliating, and then it dragged my family into this. I confronted Adam, and he admitted it and cried, so of course, I fell for it and forgave him.

Over time he would make comments about me being chubby or me having a double chin. He would pinch my stomach fat or make little comments that made me feel stupid. Then he would say that I don't have any common sense and just belittle me all the time. It made me feel that I would never be okay without him, so I needed to make this work. He would drink a lot and be taking pills. It would make his behavior so unpredictable. Mary liked "slim jims," and I would find them in his car; they would be right out in the open. She wanted me to find them. I would ask Adam who they belonged to, even though we both knew. He would deny it and say, "You're so insecure; you act like your crazy." That, my dear, is mental abuse and a tactic that abusive men use to control. I was being controlled, and I was stuck.

The prank phone calls were still going strong. When I would answer, she would just make weird noises and laugh. Adam and I were at a party at our friend's house, and Mary kept calling Adam's phone over and over and over. He would go outside and talk, and I knew it was her; I would ask, and he would say, "Don't worry about it." I'm a pretty calm person, but my temper was brewing, and I was at my wits' end. He told me to stay inside, and I said no. Mary was in her car parked outside the apartment we were at. I walked over to her and started to ask her why she was there. She would make weird noises and hit the gas and then the brake over and over again so I couldn't talk. I snapped and reached in and was going to grab her. She pulled away. I was so hurt, embarrassed, and angry. I walked back up to the apartment, and there were a few people outside watching the train wreck. Adam came up to me and said, "I told you to stay in the house." What am I, a dog? That is certainly how I was being treated. I said, "No, you don't get to tell me what to do." He forcefully grabbed me by my shoulders and went to shove me into the apartment. Adam had a friend named Jeremy that was much taller and stronger than Adam. Jeremy grabbed Adam and said, "That's not how you treat women." Adam had nothing else to say, and he walked away. That act of kindness gave me strength that day.

Things went per usual; he said he was sorry and cried, and I forgave him—over and over again.

I am so ashamed of who I became. I wouldn't be truthful if I didn't tell you all this part. We were at another party sometime later, and Mary had left her car at the house we were at. We had been drinking, and I keyed her car—not a little scratch, I keyed it really bad; Adam and another person that was there did as well. It was awful. The repercussions were awful, too; she put sugar in my gas tank and spray-painted my house. Well, she didn't do it herself; she had someone else do it. That was not me. I like calm and peace, and I am kind. What kind of monster was this making me into?

Over time Mary quit coming around—at least that I know of. Things got better than they had been. He would still go out and party and come home late. We lived by an Applebee's, and Adam and his friends were there and had lots of drinks, which ran up a large bill. They knew the server, and she also knew me. They all left without paying this huge bill! So it's very late, at least midnight, and I was sleeping. They all come in stumbling around, and one of them knocked over my Christmas tree, breaking my glass ornaments. Then Adam comes into the bedroom, flips the light on, and we had one of those large plastic pop bottle piggy banks. He starts shaking it, and change is flying everywhere, and then my phone rings. It was the server from Applebee's. She told me that Adam needs to come back down and pay his bill. I was so angry, embarrassed, and over this mess. The bill got paid, and I went to bed very angry that night.

The emotional turmoil was overwhelming me, and anxiety and depression were setting in. I was drowning and getting tired of just treading water. I really wanted to start cosmetology school, but I would have to work at night so I could go to school during the day. I couldn't be around at night because I didn't trust him. It made me resentful of him. I started to grow cold toward him. I knew that I couldn't spend my life with him; it would be a miserable life if I did. I didn't know how to change my situation. It sounds easy, right? Just leave, and it's over. There was so much more to it; emotionally, I was turned upside down. I was so emotionally frozen, and I couldn't see the forest through the trees.

Nearly every day, he would go to Wings, etc., and have lunch. There was a bartender there—let's call her Amy. She was quite a bit older than us and very pretty. She was so nice. We would meet her for lunch sometimes, and we would all talk. It seemed normal; I didn't think anything of it. Then he kept talking about Amy all of the time. He went and picked her car up at work and changed the oil for her. He didn't offer this information, and I had to overhear a conversation. The red flags were waving all over the place. He said, "It's no big deal; it's just an oil change. You're jealous of everyone; quit acting crazy." I had started to think, *Am I overreacting? Is this normal?* Trust your gut, my friends; it never lies. My gut said no, yet my mind said, "Maybe this is normal. Maybe I can make sense of it."

A while later, I was getting out of his truck, and I saw a very long blond hair, just like Amy's or Mary's. I asked him, "Whose hair is this?" Now I will admit this does sound crazy; I was not looking for hair or any evidence that a woman has been in his truck; it was just in plain sight. He said, "Wow, you are actually crazy." He had no clue where the hair had come from, but I knew it was most likely Amy's.

I broke up with him. I put on my "big girl" panties and did it. I was so distraught. He told me that I was crazy and that I just wanted a reason to break up with him. I stayed true to myself, at least for a little while. I moved home, quit my job, and laid on my parents' couch for a month, and cried and cried. The only thing I could eat was spinach dip and French bread. Do you remember that little house that Heather and I lived in? I moved back into it. I had nearly no contact with Adam for a while, then I started to wear down, and I would talk to him. He was very persuasive and told me that he knew he was wrong and he's so sorry and not to throw away all the time we had together. He begged me to meet him, and I did. We met at a restaurant, and I sat there trying to sip coffee in between crying spells. We decided that we would talk, but that was as much as I could do at the time. I was so ashamed that I even met him; It was so unfair to myself. My parents were going to be angry with me. This would hurt them so badly, so I hid it from them.

I stayed with him. I was a broken fool. We fought, and I said it's over, but it wasn't; it never was. I was weak, and he was persistent and manipulative. Now Adam wanted to get married. He didn't want to get married; he knew *I* wanted to get married—well, at one time I wanted to marry him. I knew I couldn't get married to him; I couldn't marry someone like my father. I couldn't do that to my future babies.

That is when the game changed for me. I knew I was too weak to do it myself, but I had future children to think about. I didn't want to see their mommy crying and being mistreated and abused. I know what that felt like because I saw it and lived it.

We got engaged; he thought that would keep me around. It did for a while, but my mind had been changed, and I knew I couldn't go through with it. I just had no clue how to get out now. One day Adam said, "Meet me at my parents' house at six, and we will go to Olive Garden for dinner." I said okay, and I got there about that time, and he wasn't there. I called him, and he said that he was golfing and that the people in front of them were slow so that he would be a little late. No biggie, I thought; it seemed normal. He would golf regularly. His sister and dad, and stepmom were in the house. I said I was hanging out with them. Some time had passed, and I called again, and he said, "I'll be there soon, I promise." So I waited, and then his sister said, "Come outside with me." She told me that he was with Amy at her house. She said, "I can't let you sit and wait like this." I was in sheer shock, although I shouldn't have been.

Then he pulls in, in the driveway. I asked him how golf was. He said, "Not good; I got a pretty bad score." I asked, "Is it because you weren't golfing?" His eyes filled with anger, and he was instantly mad at his sister. I told him, "It's not her fault; it's just the truth." I said once again, "We're done; this is enough." He stormed away, and I stupidly followed him; a part of me wanted to have him in front of me so I could yell at him. I wanted to get it out. I followed him to Texas Roadhouse, where he ordered a beer. He said, "Follow me to my parents' house, and let's talk about this." So I did. I stuck to my guns and said, "It's over; I can't do this anymore." He tried to explain that it was no big deal, and it didn't mean anything. The more I said, "No, I'm done," the angrier he got. Then he grabbed me and threw me to the ground, banging my head against the floor. I yelled for help, and his stepmom tried to help. He jumped up and ran out. I left his house and went home.

It wasn't long before the phone calls started and the apologies. I was done this time. I was broken, but I was done. I was really good friends with his cousin, and her dad lived close to Adam's family. She, my friend, and I were going to go out that night. I was at his cousin's house, and he must have seen my car. The phone calls started. "I bet you are going out tonight, aren't you? We need to talk." I said no. My mind was made up. We all went out that night and had a blast; then, on our way home, his cousin got pulled over, and she had been drinking. They asked for all of our identifications. I had the fake one that I was still using, so I decided I'd rather be an underage drinker than commit fraud. I gave him my real license, and they walked away.

His cousin was now in the cop car, and my friend was in the back seat crying. We had all had some drinks that night; the officer came to my window and asked what we were doing that night. I just told the truth and was unsure what the punishment would be, but I knew it was coming. He asked me if I could drive, and I said yes. He said, "Okay, I'm going to walk you around to the driver's side. Go home and don't get pulled over." I couldn't believe it! We got off scot-free. I knew we had to get his cousin out of jail, and I didn't know what to do. I had never been arrested or had any kind of circumstance like this before. So I went to her dad's house, got into my car, then pulled up to the garage, and I saw headlights behind me. It was Adam; he blocked me in. There was no way out. I realized that there were no lights on in the house. Her dad's not home; he started banging on the window and telling me to get out. My friend and I were huddled in toward the center console to get away from the windows. Then I got so angry, I got out, and I was ready to stand up for myself. He took my keys and threw them. I realized how out of his mind he was, and I wasn't going to argue with that. So I found my keys and got back in my car. He kept screaming and banging on the window until he broke it out, right in my friend's face. She started screaming and crying. He ran off, and I drove away quickly. I was scared and mad and overwhelmed. Then I saw headlights coming up quickly behind me. Adam was trying to run me off the road; he would get in front of me and slammed his brakes on, trying to get me to ram into him. He didn't stop until I got to a gas station and pulled up in front of the door. Then he sped off. I called my dad and told him I was on my way home and what had happened. Adam and my dad did not get along, and I was scared he would try to do something to my parents. The police came, and I had to tell them what happened.

This had to be it, right? Guess again! I had no contact with him for a while, and then I started talking to him again. It was very short-lived, and then it was truly the end. I wanted to fix him, to help him. Girlfriends, you cannot fix a person. Save yourself the heartache, and don't delay the pain.

Chapter 8

What I Would Tell My Teenage and Twenty-Something Self

Dear sweet girl, have no shame about who you are or where you came from. Remember that it takes strength to move on after trauma. Don't be disappointed that you're different. That will work for you later on in life, I promise. There is the only one you, the world, needs who you will become. You will become her in stages—some things you just can't rush. If I could give you some advice, I would say, "Don't worry." It's easier said than done, but whenever you feel that burning pit in your stomach and you start to worry, stop where you're at and give it to Jesus. Tell Him out loud that you trust Him. Then move on. Live your life one day at a time. We have grace sufficient for today, not yesterday or tomorrow. Yesterday's grace is already used, and tomorrow's is not given yet. Just like manna, we get it when we need it; we can't store it or stockpile it. Jesus knows what we need, and He will care for you; just trust Him and save yourself years of torment, stress, anxiety pills, cigarettes, and stress-eating.

You're going to search for what feels normal, but your normal will never be the same. You're different, altered, but just as good. Your new normal is you with your new experiences and a new strength about you. You know what hurt looks like, and you can pick a hurting person out of a crowd, and you have the desire to help them. You can go straight to someone's level and get in the pit with them, love them, and draw them out. I believe this is a gift that God has placed within you. Without the trauma and pain you have been through, would your gift be as powerful? I don't know, but I believe that God uses all parts of your life for His glory. The thing that you have been through may qualify you to do what you want to do later.

I am the thirty-four-year-old version of you, sweet girl, and still, as of now, I can promise you that God will replace everything that you have lost. He will replace it and work it for His glory. You did lose your grandma and your dad and were plucked away from everything you knew. That was painful, but He has replaced it with a better life and a new dad. You will make plans, but God goes before you and makes your path. Sometimes, you may get off the path when you feel frustrated, angry, and confused; that's a good sign you have taken a detour. Just stop where you are and ask God to put you back on His path. He is waiting with open arms and all the grace and forgiveness you could ever need.

Seeing your mom be abused left a scar. Don't worry about hiding that scar. Wear it with pride because you are a warrior, as is she. That is part of your story. Just remember you are not her protector; God is. To be the protector of another human is a heavy job. You are a mother to your son; you're not a mother to your mother. For as long as I can remember, you have worried about her; it was a valid fear for many years. Now it's a habit, so let that go. God had healed her and put her safely on a rock; she needed your dad, you needed your dad. God replaced what was lost, provided everything you needed, and protected you from things you didn't even know about. Go and be free and happy; live as though you have never been hurt.

Don't wear a mushroom cut. I know it's a little late in the game for that now, but I had to address the elephant in the room. Never lose your sense of humor. Not everyone will understand your jokes, and you're not really that funny, but you can plan an epic prank, and you're slightly ruthless when it comes to that. Your uncle Scott will try to outdo you when it comes to pranks, and he will never win. Uncle Jeff will forever be the instigator of food fights; then, we will sit back and watch the shenanigans take place.

Let's talk about food, shall we? Eating disorders are so rampant in this world. Body image is something that will be an issue for you. It will steal your joy, make you cry, and you will become obsessed over it. Then when you let your guard down, you will allow yourself to stress-eat. Then you will gain weight and feel so ashamed; you will want to avoid pictures and social situations. You will wrap your self-worth around the way you look. I promise you that no amount of new clothes, new hairstyles, or makeup techniques will fix this. They're only bandages. Lipstick won't fix that. Don't be discouraged, sweet girl; you will beat this once you make peace with food.

Food is good; it is meant to nourish our bodies and minds. We have to have it. When it is misused and is ingested to reduce stress and give temporary pleasure, it will backfire, and you will gain weight. When you want to stress-eat, chug some water, go jogging, paint your nails, read a book. Divert your thoughts from food. On the other hand, don't let yourself get too hungry; your self-control is not strong when this happens. It's much easier to resist the cookies when you're not hungry. Have your meals planned, and never be caught out without a healthy snack option to tide you over. If you fail to plan, you plan to fail. Once you gain a healthy relationship with food, you will be free.

Sweet girl, you can do anything you put your mind to, don't ever let anyone tell you differently. They don't know what you're made of. They don't know what you have seen, felt, fought through. They may look at you and base it off earthly knowledge, but you are a child of God, and His plans are bigger and better than ours. His ways are something that we can't comprehend. When you have an overwhelming desire to do something, I believe that God put that desire in you. Don't reason it away. I believe you will still get to it, but why waste years of your life in limbo, years dreaming and wishing? Spend those years believing and doing. Don't dream and wish, believe and do. Never let anyone hinder you; some people want to drag you down because it makes them feel better.

Don't wrestle with a pig, or you will both get dirty; the only difference is the pig likes it. Girlfriend, don't spend time in the company of negative people that don't wish you well. Here's another thing: if they spend all of the time there with you talking about someone else, chances are you're next. Be aware of these people; you are kind-hearted, and sometimes that is confused with being weak or a push-over. Girlfriend, you are no doormat. You are an empath, you feel people's pain, and you want to help them fix them. Those are some of the qualities that you were created with. It must be reined in; you must protect yourself from those who drain you, suck your time, and don't wish you well. You only have twenty-four hours in a day; use them wisely and keep good company. They say that you are the combination of the top five people that you hang out with. Check yourself often and remember that saying no is okay. It's not mean or rude.

Don't be so quick to give yourself away; not everyone is on the same page as you. Adam wasn't a horrible person. He just wanted to party and not have only one girlfriend. You wanted a wholesome relationship and wanted to settle down. You thought you could change him; you don't ever make this mistake again. You cannot change a person, and that's selfish if you are trying to change a person to suit you. If you have to beg a man that is supposed to love you for something, he doesn't love you. He's not that into you; have some self-respect and don't drag on. It won't end well.

Don't wait to live your life until *something else* happens. As a grandma, Mary would say, "Life is not a dress rehearsal." Live your life where you are, how you are. Don't wait until you are thinner, your hair is longer, until you have a perfect life, until you're married, until you have a baby. This isn't real; you will spend many years waiting and chasing, waiting and chasing. Don't beat yourself up over this. What's done is done; sadly, you did lose a lot of life than you could have been living in the moment. Hopefully, you will learn from this. I pray that someone else can benefit from it and not make the same mistake. If this can just reach one person, then it will not be in vain.

You don't have to prove your worth. Did you hear me? Girlfriend, you will hustle for your worth; you will hustle hard. You will work until you can't see straight, then you will work some more. You will forget to rest and have fun. You will get tunnel vision and work so hard that you work yourself into panic attacks, and your anxiety level will be so high that you keep a stomachache and are just miserable. This is a choice; this sense of chasing your worth is based on a lie that you believe about yourself. This is a stronghold in your life. You feel like you have to work harder to be as good as other people around you because of what you're trying to hide about your childhood. This makes me sad writing this— sad because I know how long this will have a hold of you. This is a choice that no one can make for you; no one even knows that you're thinking about it. You will overcome it; you will realize that this is who you are. Your worth is in God; you are the daughter of the king of the universe. You will put on your crown and hold your head up high.

Life is a mixed bag of beautiful, ugly, and everything in between. You can't pick what's in your bag, but you can choose how you react to it or how you accept it. Life is a beautiful ride, and it's full of hills and valleys. Learn to dance in the rain and cast your cares to the lover of your soul.

Comparison—it's the death of all good things. How can you compare the sun and the moon? They both shine in their own time. Don't compare yourself to someone else; we are all made up so differently. That person that you catch yourself thinking, "Wow, her life must be so easy, so great, so [insert whatever your thinking here]." You never know what someone may be battling in secret or what their home life is like. You never know.

Don't carry guilt, do not accept it. You will make mistakes in your life and have regrets. They will not outweigh all of the things you have done right and what you are proud of.

Shame, this is a big one. I could dedicate a complete chapter and out the S-word. I despise it to my core. Shame is best friends with comparison and guilt. If I may make a nerdy analogy, they're like the mean girls. We don't sit at that table, so don't let these things reside inside of you. So first off, if you compare yourself to someone, you will compare the most difficult or least favorite part of yourself with their very best quality. That makes sense, right? I hope you're sensing my sarcasm. Then you will see how those qualities that you are comparing don't measure up. Then you will feel guilty for not doing what you should have to attain the other person's quality. For example, "Wow, she is so smart and is in her third year of college. If I would not have dropped out of college, I would only be a year away from being done." Here's another: "Wow, she really manages her finances well and has made a lot of money. She can afford to pay for her family's vacation. I wish I would have managed my money well, and I could have done that for my family too." Then the guilt comes. "I let my family down." Then after guilt has sat for a while, it makes itself at home, gets nice and comfortable, then shame likes to creep in and join the party. Misery likes company.

After we have believed it for a while, it becomes a part of us. Sidenote: Sometimes, we have a valid reason to feel guilt; when guilt is real and valid, it may be there to help us change behavior or prompt us to apologize to someone we may have mistreated or hurt. More times than not in my life, guilt has been a lie. Don't get me wrong; I am as far from perfect as you can imagine, but most of the guilt I have felt has been a lie. After the guilt has settled in and we believe the lie about ourselves comes shame. Ugh, just the word *shame* can pack a punch. I have felt shame many times in my life. So let's go back to the scenarios above: "She is in her third year of college, and I dropped out." So there is the comparison, then comes the guilt for dropping out, then we believe that we are not as good as the person that we're comparing ourselves to; we believe it, and it becomes a part of us, then we have shame for failing and coming up short. Shame is sneaky and slick; when were ashamed, we don't want to tell anyone what we're dealing with, so we sit with it alone, and it has its way with all of our thoughts and impressions that we have on ourselves.

Shame is the start of a stronghold in our life. Another way shame can enter our minds is by someone telling us something that isn't true, such as "You're never going to be good enough," "You should just stop because you will never reach that goal," "You're unlovable," "Shame on you, that's your fault." Sadly the list goes on and on. Do you have areas in your life that you have shame? I am here to tell you that you can be free from this. The enemy uses these to gain control of your thoughts and how you view yourself. If he can keep you down and not see the true potential that you have inside of yourself, then he has won. If you have breath in your lungs, then I can assure you that God has a plan for your life; He has a purpose for you. Believe in yourself enough to fight against these strongholds. Forgive yourself, girlfriend.

How do you fight against a stronghold? You fight on your knees in prayer. Ask God to show you what strongholds you have in your mind. Ask Him to reveal them to you, then pray over them. Go boldly before the throne of God as a chosen daughter or son and ask for God to tear them down. Speak peace where lies have prevailed. Be healed and be free. Protect your thoughts, be mindful of everything that you are thinking and saying, speak and think life into yourself and those around you.

> Death and life are in the power of the tongue:
> and they that love it shall eat the fruit thereof.
> (Proverbs 18:21 KJV)

In closing this chapter, I want to tell you, girlfriend, that healing starts from the inside out. If you work with God and the Holy Spirit to heal your mind, break down strongholds, then and only then can you truly be healed? A lot of pain and misery that we experience is because of thinking and saying negative things. Don't be discouraged if this takes some time; I still have to remind myself to "check myself," what am I thinking and saying? Know the truth about yourself, and you won't easily be misled again.

Chapter 9

My Soul Mate and Moving to the Country

A couple of weeks after Adam and I broke up, I had gotten a phone call from Jeremy. Remember him? The guy who saved the day at the party? Well, he had been patiently waiting to ask me out on a date when I became a single gal again. By the way, I was treated, he knew it shouldn't take long. He had called my friend Katie and asked if it was too soon to ask me on a date. Now, gals, I was ready to be alone forever. I was convinced that all guys were pigs—well, except for my dad. I would just be a single gal. I did not need a man, and I was going to be an independent woman. I was going to start school and get on with my life. Or so I thought. I agreed on the date. After all, Jeremy was always such a great guy, warm and friendly, not at all a jerk, easy to be around, and trustworthy.

I told my mom and dad about the date, and they were so excited. Mom took me shopping for a new outfit. I got Express's white strapless tube top, and she told me that it looked like I was wearing a pillowcase. I disagreed and wore it anyway (she was right).

The day of the date rolled around quickly, and we hit it off so well. We sat down and had dinner and two drinks. You guys, we were there for five hours! Can you believe that? I had found my soul mate and my best friend. I didn't know it, but I would find out soon enough. He was such a gentleman; he bought me dinner and walked me to my car. Did I mention he was super-hunky? Well, he was; and spoiler alert, he still is.

Jeremy and I have been married for almost twelve years now. I know that God works all things for the good of those who love Him. If I had never met Adam, I most likely would not have met Jeremy. Okay, back to the beginning. Jeremy lived in Niles, Michigan, with one of his best friends, Jimmy.

I lived at home with my parents in Edwardsburg, Michigan. We lived about twenty-five minutes from each other. We would get together and laugh and laugh and laugh. I knew I was safe with him; he saw the good in me, not the flaws. When he would look at me, I could see the love in his eyes for me. I've never in my life had a connection to another person like I do with Jeremy. I know without a doubt in my mind that he always has my back and would never betray me. There still are some good men. He proved to me that all men are not pigs.

The day of our first date, he was super-nervous; his friend Jimmy was home, and the cable guy was working at their house. Jeremy's and Jimmy's rooms were on opposite ends of the house. Jeremy kept trying on different outfits, but he didn't have a body mirror in his room. So he was running from one end of the house to another while explaining that he has a date and needed Jimmy's mirror. This still makes me giggle. One of the first few dates we had was at his house. He wanted to make me dinner; he made his very delicious "chicken stuff." It's chicken breast, stove-top stuffing with butter and cheese slices. It's like heaven in your mouth. So delicious. I thought it would be nice to bring a bottle of wine to have with dinner. So I did, but I didn't bring a wine opener. He didn't have one, but he had a pock-etknife, so I thought, *That will work.* I opened the pocket knife up and stabbed the cork with it. Now I assumed the blade was locked; it wasn't, and I firmly twisted it and brought the blade down right on my finger. I looked down and saw a purplish-blue gash, and then it started to pour blood. It made my knees weak, and I got nauseous. Jeremy was concerned and was asking if I was okay. I played it cool and said, "Oh yeah, I'm fine; I'm just going to go wash it off in the bathroom." I walked into the bathroom and put my hand over the sink, then it happened. I folded like a cheap card table; I passed out in the bathroom. He heard a thud and a sliding sound. I was up against the wall on the floor, unconscious. He ran into the bathroom and found me; he started talking, and I woke up. I was mortified, and he was freaked out. Now, if that wouldn't scare a guy away, I don't know what would; I nearly cut my finger off and passed out in his bathroom. Hello, hot mess express. I ate the yummy dinner with my bandaged finger, and we laughed about what had happened. He also made a chocolate cake that night. I felt like a queen, having a nice meal cooked for me and not being judged for doing something ridiculous. I could get used to this.

Now we were just as happy as two people could be; the only problem was that we all had Adam's same circle of friends. It made life pretty difficult for a while. If we would go to a friend's house and Adam would show up, how awkward, right? Adam did not take this very lightly. So we had to be very strategic about where we went. One day we were at Taco Bell in our hometown, and Adam and a couple of his friends walked. They had been drinking, and Adam started making comments right off the bat. All I wanted was a bean burrito; I was so hungry. I was afraid that they were going to want to fight Jeremy. We ended up leaving with no bean burrito.

Right after that, I went down to the police station and got a restraining order. I hated to do it; it seemed cruel for some reason, but it was exactly the right thing to do in hindsight. People need boundaries, and it's never okay to allow someone to mistreat you or keep you from getting a bean burrito. Okay, I poke fun, but I really mean it. It's okay to draw a line in the sand and say, "This is it, don't cross it." I was quickly granted the restraining order. Things did calm down after this a bit, but we were forced to draw away from our friends. If we were there and Adam showed up, it would be drama and who knows what else. We were with our normal friend group less and less. I started to reach out to my old friends, and Jeremy had a diverse group of friends, so that shift happened. We were each other's best friends and did mainly everything together; this time, it was different. It wasn't out of control or mistrust; it was because we had so much fun together.

My family loved Jeremy; he was a breath of fresh air to them. He was around all the time and fit right in. A short time after we started dating, he took me down to meet his family; they live a couple of hours south. They were warm and friendly. He has a lot of siblings; I thought that was so cool because I don't have any. Sidenote: As I'm writing this chapter, my sister-in-law Mandy is sitting at the table with me drinking coffee. I know it sounds a little crazy, but after two weeks, I knew I would marry him. I've heard that saying: if you know, you know. I just knew. The crazy thing was that I wasn't looking; I wasn't desperate for a man. I didn't even plan on dating anyone for a long time. He just came into my life and was different from anyone I've ever met. We complement each other so well. I'm high-strung, and he's so calm. I've never met a calmer person than him. He is the yin to my yang, the peanut butter to my jelly. Six months after we started dating, we decided to move in together and move to Nappanee. It was about forty minutes away from our hometown; I was still living with Mom and Dad. I had to tell my dad again that I was going to move in with my boyfriend. This time was different in my heart because I knew without a shadow of a doubt that I was going to marry Jeremy. It still broke my dad's heart; he was so disappointed that I was living with a man without being married. He refused to come over to our apartment.

Nevertheless, I went; I felt so guilty, and I visited a couple of times a week. Our little apartment had one bedroom and one bathroom; the living room was a good size so was the kitchen. The tile on the floor reminded me of a gymnasium. It was also very affordable, so that was right up our alley. Our living room had a blue camel-back couch that was given to us by Jeremy's dad and stepmom, Meg. Most of our stuff was a hodgepodge of extras from my parents' house and my first round of living at the cottage house. Jeremy had some things that he really liked and definitely had an idea of how he wanted things to look. I have always been very much into decorating and had an idea of how I want our home to look. So next to our blue camel-back couch were two pictures of dogs playing poker. I despise these pictures. They would be good in a man cave, but not in our living room. There was a bookshelf that had some picture frames and books adorned the shelves. One day, we went to Hobby Lobby to look at house décor, and Jeremy found this black-and-red Oriental vase. This honestly may have been our first disagreement. It may have gotten a smidge heated; now, when I mean heated, it means I have a small tantrum and get snappy, and Jeremy gets quiet and pouts. So Jeremy wanted this vase, and I said, "That doesn't match anything we have." Then he said, "What do you mean? It's a vase; we can just stick it on the bookshelf?" He was puzzled that this was even an issue, and I was puzzled that he would want this atrocious item in our home. He pouted and said, "Why can't I pick anything out?" I tell him to get the vase. It sat on the bookcase, and I looked at the ugly thing for a whole year. One other time, I had asked my mom to come over and help me decorate the kitchen. She was happy to do so, and she brought over some raspberry-pink toile dishes and a tea-pot set. We put them on the top of the cabinets to give the kitchen a facelift. Jeremy also did not like this; he sat on the couch and did not look amused. It would take years, but I would eventually wear him down and do whatever I wanted to the house. In all honesty, though, I was finding my style, which I'm pretty sure I didn't truly find until I was about thirty years old, and I wanted him to love our home and be happy to be in it. My home and how I keep it was and still is such a big part of me. I am a homebody, and my home is a place of refuge of the solstice. It certainly took some time to mesh our styles together and a little convincing on my end.

Our little home was filled with love. Jeremy loved to cook. We spent all of our time together, talking, laughing, and being goofy. We were happy and in love. We were just content being together. We felt safe with each other; we didn't have to try to pretend to be anyone else. We took each other as we were, not trying to change one another. We only saw the good in each other; we didn't even notice our faults. We had a cat; her name is Daisy. She is still alive and well and lives with my parents. Her name has evolved to Missy Rue Rue. Isn't it funny how pets' names evolve? She is a huge, fat, and grouchy Maine coon. If you walk past her, she inevitably will hiss at you. Her grumpiness makes her even more loveable. You want to pester her to watch her have a fit. She cannot stand to have her paws touched, and she can't retract her claws. So that means that her claws will get stuck in your clothes, and she will hiss and growl, thinking it's your fault. When you try to get her claws free from your clothing, she will try to shred you like a Ginsu knife. I'm for real; the cat could be a ninja.

I went from living twenty minutes from the mall, Target, Marshalls, TJ Maxx, and Starbucks to living about fifty minutes from all of these very loved places. I was a fish out of water; though I loved the quietness and quaintness that the town offered, I didn't quite fit in. The Martin's grocery store had a tie-up for horses; the Amish folks would drive their horse and buggies there, and there would be mounds of poop everywhere. I had never seen anything like the horse-and-buggy situation. It was so sweet and quaint but so different from what I was used to.

I struggled to adjust to the area, but we sure made the best of it. There was a little video store down the road called Crystal Video. There were still video stores then, I just aged myself.

There was a delicious country restaurant close to our apartment; it was all Amish cooking. It was a great place to retreat to for a year; that's as long as we stayed. It was a great time of quiet, calm, not looking over our shoulders, and peace. That winter was very long, and we had a lot of blowing snow. The main road we lived on was long and was surrounded by trees. When the snow would be falling, it was blinding to drive in; all you would be able to see from your windshield would be white snowflakes. We spent a lot of time indoors when we were not working. Running around and visiting family and friends was not much of an option during this season. I really missed being ten minutes from my parents; I didn't like being so far away. I worked about forty minutes away, and the beauty college I was attending was about forty minutes away as well. The restaurant I was working at would schedule me to open the restaurant at 6:00 a.m. most of the time. This would have me up at the crack of dawn to ensure drive time. I was not a morning person at this stage of my life, and an early bedtime was for the birds. I sure paid for it, though. I would be dragging in like a zombie while serving up the eggs and bacon.

Winter came and went, and then we were walking into glorious spring; the birds were chirping, and the grass was green again. We were able to travel much easier, and did I mention that we were nearly swept up into a tornado? I must have failed to add that part, oh my gosh. We lived in an upstairs apartment; we could both sleep through a freight train going through our living room, and we nearly did. It was about two or three in the morning, and both of our cell phones started ringing. My instant reaction was, *Something has happened to someone!* We both answered. Jeremy's brother Chris was calling him, and my mom was calling me. To our surprise, they're asking if we're okay. "Yes, of course," we said. "What's going on?" Then we heard the tornado siren and instantly got scared. My mom said, "Get into the basement now, just run down there." So we did; there were a couple of other people there. It was our laundry room. We were all standing there in our pajamas and crazy hair. There was a huge tornado that went through our little town. It was taking a huge path of destruction. It missed us. Thank You, Jesus! It wiped out a huge part of the main town area; when the sun came up, we took a drive to see what had happened. There were fast-food restaurants torn down and buildings with their roofs lifted off. There were trees in the middle of the road and pieces of wood and metal from roofs. I've never seen such wreckage like that in real life, only on the news.

The town had come together, and we're all helping each other lift large debris from the road and helping lift limbs and such from driveways, their homes, and vehicles. Happily, to my surprise, there were no fatalities; what an awesome bunch of people, band together in a time such as that.

Chapter 10

Wedding Bells

We were sitting in the living room watching TV and folding laundry when it happened. Jeremy asked me to marry him. He got on one knee and said, "I want to ask you a question in front of Daisy (the grumpy cat)." I looked at him, and he said, "Will you marry me?" I said, "Yes!" Just like that, about six months into our relationship, we were going to get married! I was so excited, even though I already knew without a doubt that he was my future husband. Now it was going to be official; I was going to be Mrs. Rose. My childhood dream was coming true; we can buy a house and have a family. I'm a planner, can't you tell?

We planned the wedding for about six months out; we met and were married around a year after our first date. So back when we got married in 2007, there were not as many awesome things to help brides like there are now. I didn't have Pinterest or even know what it was. My main resource was magazines, so off I went. I got a big stack of magazines from Target, I'm sure. Our budget was on the smaller side, so we wanted to stretch our dollars as far as we could.

One of my dearest friends I call a sister from another mister—Melissa—let me borrow her wedding dress; it was a beautiful strapless fluffy gown. It reminded me of Cinderella. I also wore her tiara; you all may giggle now, but that was the jam back in that era. We had the wedding at the little church we had been attending; we were married by our pastor Emelio. The reception was at the VFW; my great-uncle Billy was the commander there, and we got a great deal on it. The DJ was Rich, Melissa's husband.

We got fried chicken from Martin's Super Market, and my mom's childhood best friend helped make and serve the side dishes. She was a lifesaver and hugely appreciated. Our cake was from an independent cake shop owner. The wedding colors were red, black, white, and silver. It really looked nice. The bridesmaids wore a corset-type top and an A-line skirt that flared out. They wore black kitten heels and had a red rose in their hair. The groomsmen wore a black tux with a red rose on the lapel.

The day of the wedding went off without a hitch—well, mostly; the good thing about marrying the man you love is that the details don't matter as much. My friend Mindy and I stayed at my parents' house the night before, and Jeremy stayed with his friend. On the wedding day, all the girls piled in the nursery room at the church with our dresses, makeup, cans of a spray tan, and hair spray. I had a couple of friends in cosmetology school who came and did our hair. We had a great turnout; almost everyone we invited came, and it was so humbling to see how loved we were. Once we were all ready, the pastor's wife lined up everyone, and the music started. I was so nervous to walk out in front of everyone; as I walked out, I could see Jeremy standing at the front of the church. He was nervous and red. I thought he could go down any minute. The pastor began, and we stood up in front of everyone; once he started talking, the nervousness left me. I was most likely more afraid that I was going to trip as I was walking down the aisle. We were in the home stretch now. The pastor finished our service, and the music that we were walking out to started to play. It was skipping and did not play correctly, and one big thing was missed: the pastor forgot to say, "You may now kiss the bride." We were so caught up in the music and walking back down the aisle as husband and wife that we were oblivious to this oversight. After we were married, the look on Jeremy's face was the look of a relieved, peaceful man. We were over the moon.

We stood by the doors and hugged everyone that came to share our day with us. Then we walked out, and I felt like a princess;

everyone cheered and clapped for us. It truly was our special day. We headed off to the reception. Considering that the walls were Pepsi blue and there was army decor on the walls, it was still beautiful. My mom and dad had gone there the night before and decorated. That woman can make beauty out of anything. The cake was set up, and the tables looked so pretty. People had piled in, and the reception started. Our first song was Sheriff's "When I'm with You." It was dreamy. Then the pastor spoke up and said, "Well, everyone, I forgot to tell the groom to kiss the bride," then we kissed. He also said, "Jeremy, you should have done it anyway. I don't want to have to call you tonight." I was laughing and embarrassed, but hey, we're married now, it's okay.

People stayed late; they danced, ate, and drank. It was a good party. Around midnight or so, we left and made the trek back to Nappanee to our little apartment. We were on cloud nine; we were a real married couple. I was officially Mrs. Rose. It felt good; we were young—I was twenty-two, and he was twenty-seven—and in love. We changed out of our wedding clothes and got the rest of our bags packed for our honeymoon. We were leaving bright and early in the morning. We made our way to the airport bright and early; we got on the plane, I was so nervous for the plane to take off. I had a fear of flying, and I didn't even know; fortunately, it was a small fear. I silently took some deep breaths and dealt with the internal panic on my own. Once the plane had taken off and we were smoothly sailing through the clouds, I was fine. I had not been on a plane since I was a little girl; it was so fun to look out the window and see all that was going by. We were like birds. We were going to be staying at a resort in Orlando; we had quite the list of things we wanted to do on time there. Disney World was a short distance away, and neither of us had ever been there, so we went for a day.

Magic Kingdom was truly magical; it did not disappoint. Minnie Mouse's house was so cool; I was like a kid in a candy store. Jeremy, on the other hand, was less than thrilled. About half the way through, he hurt his foot, and I had to push him in a wheelchair. He was so embarrassed, but this girl was hard-core about seeing the Seven Dwarfs and all the Disney princesses. We went to SeaWorld, which was also amazing. Our very favorite attraction that we went to was Capone's Dinner Show. If you are ever in Orlando, Florida, you should seriously check them out. No, I am not being paid to add this to my book. The resort had a Starbucks on the site and the most beautiful pool and tiki bar; we would sit out at the pool at night and listen to Jimmy Buffet.

We ate a lot of food; I'm pretty sure I packed on ten pounds during that week. It's hard to believe that it can come on that fast, but it did. We went to so many amazing dinners and walked and saw attractions. We also shopped a lot. Did I mention that Jeremy likes to shop? This fella is a shopper. How lucky could a gal be—marrying my best friend, and I now have a built-in shopping buddy.

After a week of feeling like celebrities, eating out, shopping, playing all day and night, sleeping whenever we wanted, and doing anything as we pleased, it was time to make our way back home, back to our new life as a husband and wife. We returned to our little apartment with our cat Daisy to greet us. We were excited and ready for change, with our hearts full and dreams of the future whirling around us. At least I was. I looked at Jeremy and said, "I want to move." I was ready to go back to my hometown. The year away was a wonderful break, but I wasn't going to allow any person or situation to keep us from living the life we want where we want. Jeremy said, "Okay, I'm fine with that."

We talked about it for a bit, and Jeremy was going to look for an apartment for us in Edwardsburg or Elkhart. I had another idea, though. I knew of this little cottage house—you all remember that place? Well, the price was right, and we wanted to save for a house. My sweet dad let us live there for free; we just had to pay for property tax and utilities. Jeremy was not at all happy about living there; I could understand why. I had a special place in my heart for this little house, though, and if we were going to save money and get ahead in life, we were going to need to make some sacrifices. The cost of an apartment was affordable, but all of that money could go right into saving for a down payment on a house. Since I was in cosmetology school part-time and worked part-time, I wasn't able to bring in much cash, so this helped a ton.

We moved in, made it our own. It had been left just how I had left it some years back; it just had a thick layer of dust. We went in and cleaned it, repainted it. I could write a chapter devoted on how *not* to paint a house. It literally looked like a Skittles commercial gone wrong. I take full blame for that; Jeremy was an innocent bystander. Okay, ready for this? The kitchen was bright yellow with lime-green curtains. The living room was lime green with green curtains with a black design on them. The bathroom/closet area was pink. Why would I think this is okay? I still laugh about that; the only soothing normal color was the bedroom—it was taupe. The only reason that stayed a normal color was that it matched our taupe-and-pink shabby chic duvet set. We must remember that it's okay to suck when you're first figuring things out. We all suck at the beginning. I look around now, and our home is gray, white, with touches of tan and black. It's soothing, beautiful, and exactly our style. If I weren't brave and tried things, we would not quite know what we like. Sometimes we have to find out what we do not like before we can unearth what we love, what speaks to us, and our authentic style.

Hard water—this house had the hardest water I've ever seen in my entire life. If you're reading this and you have hard water with no softener, just know that I feel your pain, and I'm so sorry. The sink, shower stall, and toilet would be stained the darkest deep orange you could imagine. Then it started to break my hair. If there's a problem, just find a solution, right? So I went down to the grocery store and got a few gallons of water; I would wash my hair with the filtered water. Then anytime I would go to my parents, I would fill these jugs. In wintertime, this would be so cold; I would take my hot shower and then grab the room temperature jugs of water and douse them on my head. The bathroom floor got cold so that the jug would feel like ice water compared to the hot shower water. The only way to clean the rust stains from the shower/toilet and sinks was to use the Works toilet bowl cleaner. This stuff is caustic, and I don't recommend any-one using it other than in the toilet. I would have to wrap a T-shirt around my face and open all the windows, even in winter. Then I would squirt it on, and as soon as the cleaner touched the surface, it would disappear. It was like a chemical mushroom cloud of fumes.

We were in the cottage house for two years; we had so much fun there. Bonfires and friends over all of the time. It was close to my parents again, and I could see them more. One Sunday, we went down to visit my brother- and sister-in-law. This day changed the trajectory of our lives; we bought Maxx home. Guess who Maxx is? He's a "beagle and Jack Russell terrier" mix puppy. He was a puppy then; he's an old man now. He was and still is so adorable, loving, protective. He was also for many years hyper and destructive he has separation anxiety. We have this joke: we can only have a pet sitter once and find another person. Maxx had made weekend getaways quite difficult. I am his person, that's it. He follows me around and is my shadow. He sleeps on my bed and won't eat until we're home.

One weekend we wanted to go to Cedar Point; weekend get-aways are a blast for a newly married couple with no kids. We wanted to get away and play as much as we could. Mom and Dad agreed to watch Maxx for the weekend; Mom was working a third-shift job at that time, so that morning would be her bedtime. We came over, and she was asleep, so we had a nice long leash and tied it to the tree to give Maxx lots of room to play since they had no fence. We knew he would bark and howl, and we didn't want to wake Mom up. This dog howled repeatedly until she got up; he was outside near her bedroom window. She went outside and got him to bring him into the house. He got away from her and ran; now, this dog could run for miles without stopping, and they lived near a road. So my poor sleep-deprived mother went into the house to get on some tennis shoes to hunt him down. She opened the door to go back out, and there he was standing at the door. She snatched him up and put him in the house. Needless to say, they never watched him again.

My old boss and friend Rocco watched him *once*. He had a nice little dog named Caesar, and we thought they would play and have fun. Caesar was very laid-back and chill. Maxx obviously was not. Rocco had some people over for an early Thanksgiving dinner. He pulled the turkey out of the oven and had it on a table in his dining room. He was in the kitchen getting sides ready, and then *it happened*. Maxx was at the table looking at Rocco and eating his turkey. Another one bites the dust.

Maxx was a hard dog, to say the least; he would eat my shoes and get in the trash and bark incessantly. We loved him too much not to keep him, so life with Maxx continued. We would try to get dog-friendly hotels and bring him with us, but he would bark and howl that whole way there, and it made you want to get out of the car. After a while, we just decided it's easier to make day trips. One early morning, he took off running, and I had to go to work. He was gone; I was home alone, and it was still dark out. I heard dogs barking way over in the field, I made my way out there in the dark cold trying to find Maxx; I searched and searched. I'm walking back to the house, and I'm unsure what to do. Then he's sitting right by the door. *This dog will be the death of me*, I think to myself.

At the time, it was overwhelming; but as I look back, it gave us some good stories. There were a few more pet sitters over the years, but not many. He still likes to knock the trash over and strew trash all over the house; he still barks a lot, but in the end, we love him, and he's been a part of our life for a long time that we don't know what it's like not to have him. Other than a short time when my brother-in-law Robbie had to keep him for some time because he was acting out when our son was born, but that's another story.

That was us—all three of us in that tiny little cottage, as snug as a bug. Did I mention how easy it was to clean and maintain that house? Even with a dog and us, I could clean the whole cottage in about a half-hour, and I mean deep clean. That little place gave us time to have fun, play, and make memories. It served me well both times I lived there. Its quaint little charm left an impression on me, even when I was desperate to move on and buy a home of our own.

Chapter 11

House Hunting and Adulting

It was about two years after we had first moved into the cottage, and Jeremy had been working really hard to build his credit up so we could buy a house. At that time, my credit was awful; the same day I turned eighteen, I went down to the mall and opened two credit cards, one for PacSun and the other for Express.

I mean, who in their right mind gives an eighteen-year-old person a credit card? I have the answer for that: the credit card companies do. So I got the credit cards and basically maxed them out immediately. The cards had small limits of about two hundred and fifty dollars, but the interest rate was through the roof. I thought to myself that it's easy, the payments will be small.

The bill came, and for some reason, I just didn't pay it. At this stage of my life, I am an overly responsible person. To think back at this girl I used to be is so strange. So then the late fees came rolling in, and guess what? I still didn't pay it; who was I? Letters started coming to my parents' house addressed to me; that totally busted me out. My parents started asking questions about what it was, and I finally told them. My dear dad came to the rescue; he was not at all happy about what I had done, but he drove me down to the mall to pay the bills at the store.

When we arrived, they pulled the bill up, and they said, "I'm sorry, you can't pay the bill here anymore because it's been turned over to collections." I was crying, and my dad was not happy. So at the ripe old age of eighteen years and a few months, I have now ruined my credit; at the time, it was no big deal, but it certainly haunted me later. My dad made some phone calls, and we got it paid, but the wreckage it caused would take years to fix. If you're reading this, thanks, Dad.

So back to Jeremy working on his credit score so we could buy our house. Since his credit was already better than mine, we put everything we could into his debt and worked on whipping his credit score in shape. Mine was so bad that we couldn't even my credit on the loan because it would drop his score down. We had to get a loan using only his income; it was like I didn't even exist. We were chomping at the bit to move into our own home; I was ready to nest and decorate. We met with a mortgage lender, and he said he would take a look at Jeremy's credit and see if he could help us. This took a couple of weeks for us to get a word back, so we started looking at houses in the meantime.

We were smack-dab in the middle of the recession, and there were so many homes that were bank-owned or in the foreclosure process. It was so sad to see people losing their homes; so much was lost during that period. We live in an RV factory area, and when the factory is booming, the economy is great; but when it's not, it hits hard. Lucky for us, we were living on love and didn't have enough money even to feel the recession. So the search was on; our goal was to find a foreclosed home. Quickly we found our dream home; it was just a couple of minutes from my parents' house in Edwardsburg, our hometown, and the place that we wanted to live. The schools are amazing, and the house was so cool; it had big pillars in the front of the house and a nice long driveway. As soon as I saw it, I was decorating it in my mind; *I'll put that wreath on the door. Let's paint the front door this color.* We looked into the windows and knew we just had to have this house. It had to be ours. We called the mortgage broker and asked him if he could get us a loan for this exact house. He said he could see what he could do and would get back to us. We waited, not so patiently. We were so anxious. Then one day, I was at work, and I got the call; we needed a better credit score to get the loan. We were crushed; it's been about nine years, and as I write this, I can still feel the sting from that phone call. If I hadn't ruined my credit on my eighteenth birthday, this wouldn't have happened; that's what kept running through my head. It was the truth; sometimes, the truth hurts. We kept working on it and waiting for the credit scores to refresh and checking on the house to see if it's still on the market. It would have had a restraining order if this house was a person because we were stalking it. One day it happened, and the investor purchased the house with cash. He or she bought our house, the one that we had decorated and made plans for, the one just down the street from my parents and in our hometown. Yep, that house, and we were crushed. It was official: the house was gone.

After a little time had passed, we started looking again; nothing would ever live up to that house.

That's what it felt like, at least. We slugged along, paying off all the debts we could and worked on the debt-to-income ratio. We would look at houses but didn't want to get too excited about anything because we didn't want the same thing to happen again. I wanted to find a way to make some extra income, so I started an online tutu and bow boutique. I made hair bows, tutus, baby shoes, and these darling little ruffle bottom baby boomers. We had very little room in the house, but I did have an ironing board that had an adjustable height. I could sit on the couch and adjust the ironing board to the height I needed. I was so happy to have this little setup. I had been making some traction and getting the skill down on how to make the bows and tutus and perfect my craft. I was so ready to have more in life and to move on, but as you know, we were stuck until that credit score was higher. I worked on a business that was something I could control. I called a popular local boutique and asked if I could speak to her. She agreed, and we set up a meeting time. I went in and brought a few of my items; she agreed to see them at her boutique! I was so happy; I couldn't even believe it. She wanted my stuff in her shop. I went straight to that craft store after and got every color and design of ribbon I could and went home to my ironing board to crate and get a larger supply of items to bring to her. Then it happened; my ironing board broke. It got stuck at the highest level it would go, so I would have to stand on my tippy toes to use it. I lost it; I wanted to throw myself on the floor and have a tantrum. I thought to myself and probably yelled out loud, "I can't even have a working ironing board!"

I felt sorry for myself for a few days. Friends, I know how silly this sounds, but these emotions were real. I could have just gone down and bought another ironing board, but it was deeper than that. I felt defeated as if I would take two steps forward and one step back.

A few days later, I was in our driveway cleaning out my car; I was in a bit of a funk. I had the radio playing, and out of nowhere, this calming presence came over me. All of the anxiety and frustration just went away, and I knew in my heart that God was making a way and that everything was going to be great—not even just okay, but *great*. He had a plan for us, and we just needed to be faithful and do what we felt Him leading us to do. That day changed the game for me. I had been striving to make things happen how I wanted them to go by my own will and strength. That was not working for me, and I needed to change the way I thought and operated. So I did; I put it in God's hands, and when I would feel overwhelmed, I would say, "God will make a way if it's meant to be. I won't worry about this, and I'll trust God." That's just what I did. It made life a lot happier, and I was a great deal more pleasant for my husband. By the way, he was calm as a cucumber the whole way through this process; he's got a gift. God knew I needed a calm husband to even me out. He always knows what's best for us.

So from there on out, I fully put my trust in God. I thought that I had put my trust in God all along, but had i really? When I got quiet and and thought about it, I had not.

Trust—the firm belief in the reliability, truth, ability, or strength of someone or something.

I said I trusted God, but my actions called me out. I was a hypocrite. If you trust in the reliability, truth, ability, and strength of God, then you do not sit and worry and try to figure it out yourself. I decided that day that I would stop the struggling, strife, and exhausting myself. I decided to stop worrying. Now, with that being said, it did not come easy. I had to choose to remind myself every day, multiple times a day, that I was going to trust God. I would feel the pressure in my chest, and my heart started racing; I would then feel defeated, overwhelmed, and sad. That was worry and strife coming over me. It had been welcome for so long. Why wouldn't it return again and again? I had to stop, remember the truth that God is a good God, and He will do the best for my family and me at the right time. Then I had to take the physical action of not figuring it out myself or having Jeremy try to figure it out. Sidenote: I do not mean just letting things happen. We did what we should do, such as work hard and pay off debts to correct our credit score. We knew what the problem was and worked for a solution but did not worry about strife. We did our part but didn't try to do God's part. A short time later, Jeremy's credit was in good standing, and we were Pre approved for an FHA loan. Just like that, the hard work and trust in God paid off.

The right house would work out for us at the right time; if it's God's will, it will happen. Soon after this all happened, I had been looking at the Realator.com app; I was doing my usual search in

Edwardsburg. Then this house popped up; it looked just like the "one that got away," but it didn't have pillars. I was really excited; the price was very good. I got super-excited, then I saw that it was in Elkhart. It was right across the state line, so I never minded it again. Jeremy soon brought this house to my attention, and I said, "It's so cool, but no way, it's not in Edwardsburg." He talked me into driving by it. We looked outside, and I wasn't sold. It was in the winter, and things were snow-covered.

We continued to look, but with no luck; nothing in our price range struck us. We continued to live and be happy where we were planted. I knew in the depths of my heart that God was working on something. When spring rolled around, the house that looked like the "one that got away" was still on the market. It was different, though. It was bank-owned, and they had replaced the windows and the flooring and painted the whole inside of the house. The price of the house had not gone up, just the quality. Jeremy wanted to go see it, and we scheduled a showing. We pulled into the driveway, and the house that I had not been that interested in before suddenly was so appealing. We went inside and looked around quickly; we were standing in the living room and looked at each other. We just knew this was going to be our home. The realtor (our aunt Danielle) asked if we liked it. We said, "Yes, we will take it."

Now one may think that we may have settled because we had waited so long; that was indeed not the case. If we wanted that house during the winter when we first looked at it, it would not have had the updated windows, flooring, and paint. That update was worth thousands of dollars and lots of time. We wanted that house so bad, and we were so thrilled to have the chance to have this house as our home. I can't tell you how excited we were. I believe that God will put desires in your heart, and He can also take them away. I believe He put that desire in my heart at the right time, the time that worked best for us, because He is good and worthy of our trust, and His ways are higher than ours.

We went down and wrote up the offer right away; we even bid five thousand over in case someone else placed a bid around the same time. We then had to wait for the offer to be accepted; then the house would have to pass FHA loan inspections, then voila, we had bought a house. Sounds easy, right? Well, there were a couple of bumps along the way. It took weeks to hear back from the bank about the loan being accepted. It took so long that we decided to start looking at other houses in case this fell through. Nothing compared to the one we put an offer on, but we went forward. The loan broker even told me that I had champagne taste on a beer budget. That kinda stung at the time, but now it makes me giggle, especially since I'm sitting in that house that we waited on as I write this book. We were unaware of this, but an investor had placed a cash offer on the house. They were going to accept that offer, but it fell through; our offer was next than one right behind us.

The phone call came one day, and we were told, "They accepted the offer! You need to come down and sign paperwork and bring $4,000 for your down payment." Oh no, we thought. During this time, the economy was down, and people were getting first-time home-buyer loans with 0 percent down. We did not qualify for zero down, and we had nothing saved. I had to call my dad; I asked him for the money, and we would pay him back. I'll remind you that he let us live in the cottage for only the property tax cost (which was very little) so we could save for a down payment. He was perplexed that we had saved zero dollars. He agreed and wrote the check but was disappointed, to say the least. Thank you, Mom and Dad.

I drove the check down and dropped it off; we were all set for inspections now. So many things could have gone wrong, but they didn't, and we closed on the house a few weeks later. The footprint of the cottage house was less than half of the downstairs. It was like moving into a huge mansion compared to where we came from. We had some friends help us move; it was an exciting day. It was like a dream. We would laugh and think about how bare the house would be because we didn't have enough furniture and stuff to fill it. We didn't care a bit, though; we were just so happy to get a better version of "the one that got away." Our dog Maxx would run on the wood floors and slide, and the echo of his nails hitting the ground filled the house. I sat down on the floor and looked around in awe of our home; it was all ours. The neighborhood was very old and established with lots of big trees; you should see what fall is like around here. Leaf removal is crazy, but the trees are gorgeous. Many people who live in the neighborhood have lived here for thirty years; they had built their houses and got puppies and had babies. Now those puppies are very old, if still around at all, and their babies are grown-up and moved away. They have history here; they are kind and come to welcome us. They were so excited that a young married couple had moved in and brought some new life to our street. We have been blessed with the best neighbors a young couple could ask for. We were planted in a great place; we started our roots here, and they quickly took root and grew strong.

Chapter 12

Homeowners

We had done it; we were in our new home. It was all ours. For the first few weeks, it seemed like it was a dream. The reality of it had not set in. Each time we would pull in the driveway, my heart would swell; we were so very proud. Even though the house had been repainted and the flooring was updated, we still had our plans. We had a vision for what we want our house to look like. Our vision changed frequently, and so did the wall color, but hey, we were finding our decor style. Our home had a colorful history; most of this we were unaware of until we moved in. Our house had been home to a drug dealer; now, let me paint a picture of this. Our neighborhood looks very beaver-cleaver. I can't wrap my head around a drug dealer living in this house. The drug dealer also was convicted of murder and was in prison. He killed a woman in her home. The thought of this makes me shudder: a murdering drug dealer lived in our home. That was a hard pill to swallow. The shed in the backyard had no doors on it and was placed on top of a cement slab. He had vicious dogs tied up by the shed, and his "goods" would be stored in the shed. I'm not sure, but it makes for a good story.

That spring, when the rain came, trash started to surface in the woods behind our home. There was so much trash. We would go out regularly and pick up as much as we could; just when we thought it was all picked up, more rain would come, and more trash would surface. It would be stuff like old pots and pans, kids' plastic toys, old tools, and plain old trash. One day I saw the sole of a Timberland boot slightly sticking up from the soil. I dug it out and looked at the shoe; it looked new. Not like a pair of beat-up workout work boots— who buries work boots anyway? I have an idea: someone who buries a steak knife next to the boots. I promise you, friends, this happened. New-looking boots and a steak knife buried next to each other in a shallow grave.

The next and last family that lived in our home was an Oriental family; their story is sad. There was a husband and wife and at least one child. The husband left the family, and the mother worked so hard to make ends meet, and she just wasn't able to. She would make homemade authentic egg rolls and sell them at her work on Fridays. The house payments got behind, and they eventually left the house in the middle of the night. Our neighbor said that he saw the front door open and came over to check on her. She and the child were gone; their things were gone, and they never returned. The house sat vacant for quite some time; a pipe froze in the kitchen during the winter, and the house flooded. This is the reason that we got all the new flooring and windows. The house had a sad past. When we moved in, I was cleaning the cabinets, and I found some bottles of Oriental cuisine-type cooking sauces, and the cabinets had layers of frying grease coating them. It was her story; it was a sad one. I wish that lady well and hope that she is making egg rolls just for its fun in her own new kitchen.

One of the first updates we did was the kitchen cabinets. They say the kitchen is the heart of the home, and I couldn't agree more. We all love to eat, right? We also all gather in close when we get home from work and school. This is the space where the coffee is brewed, the bellies are nourished, the cookies are baked, and the school lunches are packed, tucked in safely with a little note. Caring for my family and feeding them well is a direct line from my heart; it's how I show my love to them. I had to make this sad kitchen my own and fill it with joy.

The cabinets are about thirty years old and an ugly shade of brown lacquer. I wanted white cabinets, but replacing them was not in our budget at the time. So I scrubbed the oil and finger smudges off and got to work. First, I went to the basement and laid a big roll of plastic down; I took the cabinet doors off and numbered them so I would remember where they belonged. I took the old hardware off and tossed it. Then I lightly sanded the brown beasts, wiped them down, and applied primer and white paint layers. Not so bad, I thought...think again. The cabinet doors were a total nightmare. I would do a coat a night, let them cure overnight. Then I would flip them over. I did this over and over again because the brown kept showing through.

Once I was finished with the paint, I bought new hardware, hinges, and handles. It was time to hang the cabinet doors. I go downstairs and get a door, place it on the cabinet it belongs to. I get the hinge out and put it where it belongs, then I take the screw and screw it in. Bless my heart; I did not know about Pre-drilling. I was trying to put a screw into a piece of heavy-duty wood without Pre-drilling. The screw would pop off and fly across the room; I would have to climb off the counter and search for the screw, just to try the same thing again. After a few hours of this, I was sitting on the floor, crying like a toddler that spilled her milk. I called my mom, and she told me about said Pre-drilling. Game changer, for real! I went down to my husband's tool chest and found some drill bits.

It worked beautifully—until I needed to close the cabinet door; the door just popped back open. I kept closing them, thinking that for some reason, the problem would go away. Isn't that the definition of insanity? Yep, pretty sure it is. Tension, that was the problem. All of the screws had to have the same tension. What in the heck. So I found myself sitting on the floor crying, once again like a toddler. This time the toddler was having a full-blown tantrum. Jeremy fixed it, and life resumed, but, my reader, *if* you ever decide to paint your cabinets, please think that through. If we moved into a house and the cabinets were purple, we would just have purple cabinets until we could get replacements, just saying.

We did a ton of renovation ourselves and with the help of my dad. He was so helpful; he and Jeremy did the drywall of the entire downstairs area and built rooms. There were two front doors. It was a large entryway, and water could leak inside. We started searching for a new front door and found a beautiful one, and it was even on clearance. It was much smaller than our preexisting doorway. I had much faith in my dad, though; did I mention that he built Mom a house? With his bare hands, can you believe that? He worked night and day—I mean that literally. He worked a day job then worked at night. He did this for quite some time, and then it started to wear on him. So he quit his day job and worked on the house until completion. So I knew he could make the oversized doorway smaller and make the door fit. And he did just that. He saved the day once again.

We were ready to start our family; we were waiting to get the house in order first. I didn't want to be painting and lifting heavy things while our precious bundle was in the oven. So we really hit it hard; we would stay up until the wee hours a night on the weekends. We were on the right track, and then it happened. Jeremy lost his job. This was so hard. I had all of the anxiety built up about being a homeowner. We had a huge list of materials to buy and projects to do, let alone paying for the actual house. It put so much pressure on me. Jeremy felt so bad about it, but there was nothing we could do. He started looking right away, but the economy was down, and jobs were scarce. He was and still is a delivery driver; it's what he has done for the last twenty or so years. When those jobs aren't turning up, he tried a few other things; he hated them but would stay at them until he could find another job.

Our plan was to start trying to get pregnant on New Year's Eve; it felt as though we should postpone it due to the current situation. I felt so much pressure being the sole breadwinner, even if it was for a short time. I was a newer stylist at a really popular hair salon; that really helped me during this time because my clientele grew quickly, and we stayed afloat. Granger Community Church was our home church; they were offering FPU (Financial Peace University, by Dave Ramsey. Friends, please absorb what I'm about to tell you. If you ever get a chance to go to FPU, please, please, please do it. If you go all in and stick to it, it will change your life. Even if you don't struggle with money, it gives us a healthy respect and relationship with money. I told Jeremy about it, and he agreed to come. We were sitting in a room at GCC (Granger Community Church) at a table with a couple of other couples, watching Dave Ramsey on a large TV screen. The wisdom that this man poured out onto us is remarkable.

He and his family had gone bankrupt and built themselves back up using common sense and God's principles. He would tell us stories of what they went through during the difficult days. Dave said that his wife would make him a tuna fish sandwich every day for lunch; needless to say, he was sick of tuna fish. This class was life-giving to us. If I remember correctly, it was every Thursday; it was a nice time out together as well.

I knew in my heart that it would be okay; walking blindly through a difficult time is never an easy task. We kept walking, we kept trusting, and we just kept on. We finished the class, and let me tell you, we were hard-core about it. For those of you who aren't familiar, set a budget, and whatever you choose to spend on groceries, for example, you put that much cash into an envelope.

You only spend that amount, no matter what. You don't swipe a debit card or credit card. If you don't have the cash, you don't buy it. This method exponentially moved the needle when paying off debt and saving is your goal. It's simple, yet not easy. It's not glamorous, sometimes not very fun, but it works. I have to say that we made it a game, and it was fun, most of the time. One of the many things that we got out of this class was *peace*. Financial Peace University held to what it promised. Even with the little we had, we had peace, and we had enough. God was carrying us, and He was also teaching us a lesson if we were willing to listen. Our faith is like a muscle; the more you use it, the stronger it gets. Jeremy losing his job seemed like a horrible thing, but in hindsight (which is twenty-twenty), going through this situation gave us a complete money makeover. The way we thought about money completely changed. We changed our mindset from a place of lack and looked at whatever money we had as an opportunity to push ourselves forward to the main goal, which for us was being debt-free, completely debt-free, including our house. If this had not happened, I don't know if we would ever have been truly responsible for our finances. We learned how to manage money for the rest of our life. Jeremy losing his job was a blessing in disguise. We have been on the journey for about eight years now. I would like to say that we never strayed for a season or made any more poor money choices. If I did, that would be a lie; we have waivered.

There have been times where I was too tired, busy, or full of excuses to go to the bank and get cash out to fill the envelopes, so we would swipe debit or credit cards without ever tracking how much we were spending. There were times when I had already spent my spending money and the desire to buy that cute top from Instagram was stronger than my willpower. Sometimes Jeremy was 90 percent in, and I was 10 percent in and vice versa. But we always, always, always got back on track. Most of the time, my mindset is all-or-nothing; I wish that wasn't my natural bend, but it is. I have to remind myself that just because I went a little over on my grocery fund doesn't mean that I should just go all willy-nilly that week. Just a soft reminder: it's never too late to get back on track. Even now, as you read this, it's a new year, a new month, a new week, a new day, a new moment. Every second is a chance to start over and get back on track. Beating yourself up because you made a mistake is not productive and will not serve you well.

We have been on our journey for eight years now; we are just under two years to reach our goal. As long as we don't have any surprises in our future. This is because we kept getting back on track, over and over and over again. We had really grown up; we were homeowners, financially responsible, and were ready to start our family. We prayed on it for months; the choice to start a family was so overwhelming. The decision to bring life into this world was scary; even though we wanted it more than anything, it also scared us more than anything. All these thoughts went through my mind: What if I can't get pregnant? What if the baby isn't healthy? What if I'm not a good mom? What if…what if…what if? If I let my mind wander any further, I would have still been waiting to decide.

We decided to start trying for a baby on New Year's Eve. New Year's Eve sounded like a good time. I love a new year, a chance to write a new chapter, to have resolved with the old chapter and the old version of ourselves. It's cleansing and a time for growth. So naturally, starting the new year, being financially stable, stable in our jobs, with a lovely home, and peace in our hearts.

Two weeks after the first of the year, I felt different. I felt a little more tired than usual. I knew in my heart that I was pregnant. I took about a thousand pregnancy tests; the tests said no, but I knew different. My heart was overjoyed. I told Jeremy what was going on, and I was pretty sure that he didn't believe it. I mean, who gets pregnant that fast? This was a tremendous blessing, but it was so surreal. About a week later, I got another pregnancy test. It had two lines. That test confirmed what I already knew. I was overjoyed and showed Jeremy;

he said, "Are you sure?" At this point, I was a professional pregnancy test reader and could teach an online course about it or buy stock in Clearblue easily. Is that even around anymore? The morning sickness hit pretty quick. I adore coffee; I don't even like to joke about not having my morning two cups of joe as soon as my feet hit the floor. It made me so sick. I'm talking about full-fledged stomach flu, a type of sickness. I was nauseous and having caffeine withdrawal. The only things that sounded good to eat were carbs; I'm talking biscuits and gravy, crackers, the bread of any kind. The exhaustion that came in those first couple of months was extreme. I fell asleep on the couch holding a plate of spaghetti once; the amount of energy it takes to grow a human is no joke. Sidenote: I'm sitting at a table writing this as my son and husband sit across from me. They are doing homework. As I look at them, it is such a reminder of how good God is. I have been greatly blessed. That boy of ours was worth all of the sickness and exhaustion I went through. I would have done it twice over. For those moms out there that go through that with other little kids at home, please know that you are my hero. You are awesome and strong; you are a warrior. To those moms that are going through the adoption process or having fertility issues and are longing to have that little one as their own, stay strong. The birthing process may be different, but what happens in our hearts is very similar, I'm sure.

You know that you want to be a mother more than anything; you know that you would lay your life down for that child. Your arms ache to hold them. Stay the course, sweet mamas.

Chapter 13

I'm a Mess, Pregnant, and Desperate to Resolve

We're going to be parents! I mean, can this just happen? Don't we need a license or something? I'm not sure I'm qualified. That's not true—I was *sure* that I was *not* qualified. I knew that we would love this baby with every ounce of our being, but to be honest, I was scared. I knew that I needed healing; I wanted to be whole and healthy before I became a mother. I wanted to raise our children in a healthy way. I didn't want my wounds to bleed on him. I was scared that it would break me if I actually got to the root of my anxiety and fear. I wasn't sure if I could return mentally to what I had so deeply repressed. What I'm talking about is my childhood, my family in Kentucky. I suppressed all of it. I couldn't have one without the other, so I suppressed every aspect of it. I went back one time a couple of years after my dad died. I stayed with Uncle John and his family; I loved seeing them and had fun. But the grief was heavy. Everywhere I looked were fragments of my old life; down the street was my childhood home, the home that I lived in not long ago, and the barn and creek I used to play in. Places we would go would be places that Mamow Lowis would take me. Not to mention that I really missed my mom; being away from her panicked me. I have had that issue since I was a young child. I would make up excuses to call her from school in kindergarten and first grade. So being away from her tore me up; I just wanted my mom to be there, and she couldn't. That's not how things worked anymore. The heaviness of the grief I was experiencing was so painful and consuming. Everywhere I went, people felt sorry for me and had pity on me. I felt as if I was no longer a regular kid but a marked kid. "Oh, that's Mark's daughter. Can you believe what happened at the gas station? That's so awful. If Lowis were alive, she wouldn't have been able to handle it. That's why she went first. That poor family, one thing after another. I wonder if they're okay." But not the kind of wondering if someone is okay, the kind of wondering/asking when you just want to know the details. All I wanted was to be normal, and that was no longer in my cards. I felt like I was damaged and that my father's death was always going to be the elephant in the room, and I hated it. I hated what happened, I hated that this was my reality, and I hated that my family was torn apart and sad.

The first night, I was lying in bed with the window open; it was dark out, and all you could hear were the bullfrogs. That's when I could cry; I let it all out from the day. Crying in front of people and being vulnerable had never been something I'm comfortable with. I was surrounded by so many people but felt so alone. This place had so many good things in it, but the reality of what had happened was too much. Between the trauma of watching my mom being beaten, fighting, and the death of grandma and my father being murdered—I just couldn't process anymore. I shut down, not in a way that anyone would notice. I wasn't depressed or acting any differently. I just shut down anything in my brain having to do with my dad, grandma, and Kentucky. I blocked it all out and told myself over and over and over again: "You're okay; this didn't ruin you. You are fine." So instead of processing these emotions properly and then moving forward in a healthy way, I just shut that down. I focused on my life and current situation, tried to make myself as normal as possible, and hoped that kids didn't ask too many questions. When people would ask where my dad lived, I would tell them that he lived in Kentucky but had died of a heart attack. My whole life until probably by my early twenties, that's what I would tell people; I hid from the raw vulnerability that would bring or the possible judging. Something that I learned from running from something is way more painful and exhausting than just owning it. People would have most likely responded with compassion then moved on. I am aware that I created this scenario in my head and played it out how I think it would go. I played it out with the worst-case scenario. I can attribute that to fear, and fear, my friends, is a liar. I let fear rule me and make me live somewhat of a lie for most of my life. The truth will set you free. If I could tell my younger self that I would be one day writing a book telling everything that I spent my life trying to hide, I would not believe it. If this can reach just one woman, my mission has been fulfilled. If this resides with you, please know, you are not alone. Most of us are working harder than we should just to be something that we're not to cover something that happened to us out of our control.

You are more than what happened to you; you are more than what you are running from. This doesn't define you. Stop where you are and turn around and face whatever you are avoiding; look its square in the face. Process it, and move on. Don't spend your life running from your trauma, it's exhausting. It will be hard, and it will suck, but not as hard as never resolving it. The number of side effects of repressing issues is overwhelming, depression, anxiety, addictions, compulsive behavior, and emotional and mental disorders. The list goes on. Take a break and lighten your load; you will thank yourself, you are worth it. Your family needs the very best version of you, and if you're like me, you want to give it to them.

After that trip, I never returned. That sounds so extreme, but I just couldn't. So if I wanted to be okay at that time in my life, I felt that this was the only way. I had to stuff down this huge chunk of my life and forget for a while who I used to be, where I come from, and what had happened. My uncle John usually visited a couple of times a year, and we loved his visits.

But now, I need to start the healing process. As scary as it was, it needed to happen. I would not do it for myself, but I would do it for our child. I needed to break the cycle of dysfunction and broken-ness. I can assure you that I am not a still not a perfect parent—that doesn't even exist. But my wounds needed not to trickle down to our son, and I would do anything in my power to stop it. Even it meant I had to open a can of worms that I so badly wanted to keep closed.

So I asked Jeremy if he wanted to visit my family in Kentucky and where I came from. He said yes. I contacted my family and planned a date. I was so anxious to face what I had been trying so hard to forget for so long. Maybe this would be how I dealt with my anxiety issues; maybe this could be my deliverance.

In the weeks leading up to our trip, I struggled with the fact that if I was going to open up and try to get some healing from what so deeply plagued me, I was going to have to be vulnerable. I was going to have to admit that I was indeed broken. I was so worried about how long it would take to work through this and if I would even be okay during the process. I had no clue how I would react when I saw all of my childhood triggers and pain points. My anxiety was through the roof, and I felt so overwhelmed on where to start this melting pot of emotions that has been simmering deep beneath the surface for two decades. I needed to open the lid, and it was terrifying. I was frozen with fear and overwhelmed. Yet, a part of me was so excited to embrace all of the good parts of my life that were overshadowed by the bad: loving family members, happy memories, and good times.

As we drove down to pay our visit, I anticipated seeing all my family and introducing Jeremy to everyone. When I say *everyone*, I mean everyone. I have a lot of aunts, uncles, and first cousins, and they had a lot of babies. It was a big happy reunion. As we pulled into the "Holler," we drove past my childhood home, and I didn't even realize we had passed it. I had thought that I would have this huge feeling of gratification as we passed my childhood home on the way to Uncle John's house. I can't believe that we passed it. It could have been the fact that I had to pee so bad. You have many other options to stop and use the restroom once you got into Corbin and passed the ExxonMobil station as you enter town (where my dad was killed). Unless you want to knock on a stranger's door or pee in a field. As we pulled down the gravel horseshoe driveway, it was just as I remembered. It brought me back to running around with my cousin Nikki and sneaking green onions and playing in the hot sun for hours, and cooling off with homemade ice cream that we would sneak from the deep freezer in the garage.

Walking into the house, I felt so loved; everyone was so happy to see me, and I was delighted to see them. We started eating soon after we got there. We had some delicious burgers and visited. After a while, people started to leave; the house calmed down. We all watched some movies, and Jeremy stayed up late with some of the older kids and taught them how to properly make a prank phone call. He has refined the art of that, if I may say so myself.

As a little girl, I would go to Sammy's flea market with my mom and grandma; they had tons of booths that were filled with anything from crafts, toys, books, furniture, lawnmowers—you name it, they had it. There was a big blue metal building where you could go and get refreshments and such. I wanted to go there and see it. Uncle John told me that it isn't open anymore. I guess I had been gone for about twenty years; in my mind, time had stood still, but in all reality, things were changing. But he took me to a new one, and a bunch of us went. We shopped, walked around, and talked, then had lunch.

I could tell that Uncle John was proud that I was there; I think the sense of pride was because I was his brother's daughter, and maybe that made him feel close to his brother, and I know that he loved me. He introduced me to a lot of people; he knew everyone, and apparently, we had an even bigger family than I thought because most of them were my cousins. He would proudly say, "This is Mark's daughter Alicia." Then people would look at me in surprise, then maybe a little pity, and smile at me. The most common response was, "He really loved you." or "Bless your heart." They were all kind and most likely taken back; what do you say to the woman that you haven't seen in twenty years, and you remember her as the little girl whose dad was gunned down at the gas station? That response is something that I had hidden from for so very long, so long that I forgot that I was hiding from it. But now, things were different; I was ready for it. It was okay; I would have reacted the same way. What else could you say?

There was a booth that had flower arrangements for headstones for gravesites. Uncle John wanted to get one to put on my dad's grave. He asked if I wanted to go to the gravesite the next day. Remember when I talked about how I hated being vulnerable and crying? Well, I was about to visit that place. I knew I would be a mess, but this indeed was a step toward healing, and I knew it. I said yes; Uncle John, cousin Nikki, and her husband, Joey, all went. I never returned to the gravesite. The Hollin family has their cemetery; it was way down some dirt road. The drive was really fun; it was full of sharp turns. We were up to such a tall mountain, and there were no guardrails. To my family, this was normal; but to me, this was an adventure. It helped me get my mind off what I was about to face. As we pulled up, there were headstones everywhere—some really old, some really new, and some in between. Then I saw it—my dad's headstone. Engraved on it was "a daughter's love" next to his picture. That still tugs at my heart something fierce. Then next to it was my Mamow Lowis's and Grandpa Will's headstones with their picture. I stood there for a moment, and then it happened. The floodgates opened, and I cried and cried and cried. Maybe that was just what I needed; maybe those tears were starting the healing process. My family stood next to me and hugged me; my fear of crying and being vulnerable went away. My Southern family is a bunch of the most non-judgmental, non-condemning, loving people I've ever met. I wish I wouldn't have missed so much life with them. We can't live in the past, though, only make peace with it and move forward with wisdom.

On the way back from the cemetery, and I sat in the back seat and sobbed like a baby, I got to see the one-room schoolhouse that my Mamow Lowis and Grandpa Will went to. It was so little and sweet. If I could have picked it up and brought it with me, I would have. I was told that there were still some desks inside and that my grandpa hand-carved "Will loves Lowis" on one of them, what I wouldn't do to have that. If I were in a better mental state, I would have had them stop and let me go inside and look around and possibly take some abandoned treasures.

When we got back to the house, my aunt Debbie asked me if I was okay; that induced more tears. I said, "No, not really, but I will be." How freeing was that, to admit that I'm not okay. It was a love-hate feeling. I loved that it gave me hope that I can work through this, and I hated it because I was vulnerable. I often wonder why I hate being vulnerable so much; maybe it stems from a lack of confidence? That I have always appeared to be okay, so people didn't see the real me?

The rest of the trip was fun; we just relaxed. Life in the South has such a different pace. It's slower and calmer. I had been used to working so hard; I couldn't see straight and was always on the go. One night we all sat in the living room and shared a big watermelon; we could hear the bullfrogs outside and see the fireflies glow outside the window. It made me sad that I had let the bad win, but I was ready to take the good back. There was so much good here. The bad things that happened didn't get to steal those things too. Not if you don't let it, at least. When it was time to go home, it was sad. I hate saying goodbye. But I knew that I would be back to visit and that I had started the healing process. It felt good to no longer hide from it. The truth will set you free.

Chapter 14

Oh Boy!

You know how you see some pregnant women who are so beautiful and glowing, they just look like super-fit models who are smuggling a watermelon under their shirt? Well, that wasn't me. I was the happiest expectant mama in the world; I was also very hungry and tired. I once nearly cried because the poor teenage girl at Dairy Queen botched my chocolate-dipped ice-cream cone. I also fell asleep with a plate of spaghetti (like I mentioned earlier) and would leave at my lunch break to go to Bob Evans and get biscuits and gravy. There was something magical about that sausage gravy. Thinking about it makes me want some. Nevertheless, the pregnancy hormones are long gone, and I have a tad more self-control than I once did. I am positive that your taste buds change when pregnant. I know for sure that food tasted better to me while "prego." Maybe because once I was pregnant, I ditched the cigarettes. I smoked from the time I was seventeen…twenty-eight years old. It's such an awful habit, and if you're judging me right now, I don't even blame you. But those little white sticks had me hooked. Do you remember the commercial where the cigarettes were bullies and told the poor addicted smokers what to do? If you have ever smoked, you may relate to that; I know I sure did. I remember the first time I bought a lighter; it had a surfer guy on it, and I also bought a pack of Camel Turkish Jades. I drove a green Dodge Neon, and my girlfriends and I would smoke our cigarettes and listen to Sublime and Dave Matthews. We had our first real taste of freedom during that time. A car, a Big Gulp from 7-Eleven, and a pack of smokes—that's all we thought we needed. We were sure wrong, but we had fun along the way.

I tried to quit smoking more times than I could count; I tried and failed over and over and over again. It's amazing what you will not or can't do for yourself, but it becomes tangible when it's for someone else. I knew that I would never have a cigarette when I had a baby in my womb. It was non-negotiable. So I didn't. It was very helpful that the smell makes me want to vomit right on the spot. Smells were so amplified while I was pregnant. Jeremy still smoked while I was pregnant; he would come up to kiss me, and the smell was *awful. That is what I used to smell like? Oh my gosh, that is not good.* That was a reality check at its finest. Smokers don't smell smokers as much, but a new nonsmoker can pick up on that real quick.

Pregnancy life was going great; a few weeks in, the extreme exhaustion wore off. It was difficult to work and function during that phase, but it was reassuring that my body was zapping all my strength to take care of our baby. When that started to wear off, I got this amazing burst of energy. I thought to myself, *Wow, this isn't so bad.* I was at a Bowl of Pho with my parents. I was having this amazing bowl of seafood pho; it came with fresh herbs and was steeped in delicious bone broth. It was so good that I could eat it every day.

We had a great lunch; we went home, and it happened the next day. Hello, morning sickness. It was so bad, and it wasn't just morning sickness; it was all-day sickness. It felt like I was just about to get sick all day long. Suddenly the tiredness didn't seem so bad; I wanted to trade and give back the morning sickness. It was mine for the next six to eight weeks, if I liked it or not. The very thought of a bowl of pho made me ill. I couldn't even drive by the restaurant. The smell would, without a doubt, get inside the car. I know that I can be dramatic, but I promise this is not exaggerated. It was horrendous. The only things that tasted good were carbs and sugar. I had told myself that once the exhaustion was over, I would eat fresh, organic foods and cook a meal plan. It was so very important that I got in all of the nutrients that our baby needed. But now, if I wanted to keep anything down, it was going to be like I said before—carbs and sugar. On the flip side, they got to know me at Bob Evans. Thank goodness for prenatal vitamins and bananas.

My whole world changed; it pivoted from thinking about myself as a person to thinking about myself as a mom. What kind of mom would I be? Could I be a good mom and work? At the time, I didn't think so; I felt as if Jackson would always have a second-rate childhood if I couldn't stay at home with him. The weight of that was very heavy. I was going to miss out on so much with his life; the thought of taking our sweet helpless baby to a daycare made me want to jump off a cliff. I just couldn't do it; there was just no way. At least for the first couple of years. My wheels were turning, and I have always figured things out; I just wasn't sure if I had it in me for this one. Nevertheless, I persisted, and I didn't give up. We were a two-income family, and that's what we were used to. Losing my income would be very hard, so staying at home was not an option for us. Trust me, though, I tried to figure that out. I explored countless ways to save money for us—cooking from scratch, and I even made our laundry soap a couple of times (thank you, Pinterest), attempting to see if I could cut our budget enough to make ends meet without my income. Sadly, I could not.

On the flip side of that, I really loved what I did; I loved being a hairstylist. I had worked so freaking hard learning and growing my clientele. I had and still have a wonderful group of loyal people, but if I left for a couple of years, I would surely lose them. I would have to start over from scratch. For most of my life, I had let fear rule me; the little voice in the back of my mind seems to know your worst fears and reminds you of them as often as you can. That voice was loud, and I felt so helpless.

First and foremost, I want to be the very best mother I could be; all I have ever wanted was to be a wife and a mother. In my mind, that would also entail being a professional homemaker. I wanted to cook and clean and make our home as wonderful as I possibly could. I wanted it to always smell like fresh cooking; I wanted to always be home with our son, and when school started, I wanted to be just a call away if he needed me. I wanted to be at all of the school functions and help out in the classroom.

That was not my reality, and I had to mourn that. It hurt, and I felt like I had failed. In hindsight, I know that was a lie I was believing and that you can, in fact, be an amazing wife and mother while still working. It would take being proactive about balance and keeping my priorities straight, but you can do both and do them very well. So once I accepted that I would be a working mother, I had to make the very best of it.

My obsession was the nursery; it was my creative labor of love. I wanted everything finished and perfect. Thank you again, Pinterest; I got lots of wonderful ideas from that website. I also got a great whopping sense of how imperfect I was. What in the heck, people's nurseries look like this? We had some work to do. Do you ever do that to yourself? You know, you go online to look at home pictures of whatever you want to do, and then you're bombarded with a million pictures of perfection? Then you feel overwhelmed and defeated? I just raised my hand. If you did, too, please know that I was in the trenches with you for many years. Just to make this clear, people usually don't post their junk on Pinterest and Instagram. They post their highlights, the prettiest parts of their life, projects, or themselves. In the hopes of sharing and inspiring. For every beautiful picture you see, there is probably a big pile of clutter or useful things that made the shot look less beautiful in the corner that they moved out of the way for that shot. They may have a beautiful nursery, but they may still have a 1970s shag carpet in the master bedroom. Life is not perfect; it is messy and crazy, and beautiful. There is beauty in imperfection. My friend just took some photos for me for my blog and social media. The background of the photos looks so clean and perfect; that's because everything else was piled up on the kitchen table. I may have to put that on my Instagram. Maybe that will be good motivation for someone to not compare their life to someone's highlight reel. I wish I could have told myself that seven years ago. I'm giving you permission you to step out of the race that you never even signed up for. I challenging you to not compare your life with anyone or anything; if you really think about that and let it sink in, I bet it will take some pressure off and free you up to enjoy your life more. I know it has for me.

Back to the nursery, you guys were so fun and so pretty. The walls were gray, and the furniture was white. The bedding was gray chevron with a homemade quilt from my mom that was white with gray elephants on it. I made these amazing window boxes made out of foam board; I wrapped them in batting and covered them in the same gray chevron print. My baby shower was coming up, and I could hardly wait to organize all of his clothes in order from 0–3, 3–6, 6–9, 9–12 months. Want to know why I was so excited to do that? Because I made little closet dividers from the craft store's wooden circles, I covered them with pretty paper.

I was getting very big very fast—maybe because of all of the biscuits and gravy I was eating. I was grateful that I was pregnant during the warmer months because I could wear a muumuu. Sundresses were my best friend at the time; the thought of wearing hard pants made me shudder. One morning I went to bed, and I had a normal nose, and I woke up with a different nose. It was big and swollen like an overripe strawberry. That was something that you can't cover-up. I felt great about myself, sense sarcasm again? Pregnancy nose was real. Yet, all I cared about getting ready for our little bundle.

Our baby shower was amazing; we had two baby showers. The girls at the salon threw one for me at one of their houses. It was over-the-top—delicious food, pretty decorations, and lots of thoughtful, beautiful gifts. So many gifts, they absolutely showered me with love that day. Then when it was all over, they pulled out one last gift; it was a beautiful Coach diaper bag!

I was so excited to go home and organize that beautiful bag. I loved it so much, and it brought a little style to my new mommy world. Our other baby shower was with friends and family. It was huge; it took up a good portion of the lower level at Hacienda. It amazed me how many people showed up; I know how busy life is for everyone, and they took time out of their day to shower me with love. I felt very rich that day, and it had nothing to do with the presents.

You guys, I had enough diapers for nearly a year; my mom had put together a basket of lotions, candles, and bath products, and everyone who brought a pack of diapers was entered into a drawing to win the basket. That was amazing; people brought me the most thoughtful things, beautiful baby clothes, bath products, wipes, blankets. When I got home that day, Jeremy unloaded my car for me and was amazed at who all showed up and how loved we are. I stayed up late into the night that night putting together our new treasures, washing all of the tiny clothes, and putting diapers away in stacks. Then, of course, organizing them by size using the closet dividers I mentioned earlier. A childhood best friend and her family surprised us with a glider and ottoman. When all was put away and the room was finished, I would sit on that glider with my feet up and rocked back and forth, and I looked at the beautiful little nest our baby would come home to. I would sit and rock while rubbing my belly and dreaming of meeting our little bundle.

I decided to have a midwife and a birth plan that was as natural as possible. I wanted to try to have our baby without an epidural; if you're reading this and have delivered a baby without an epidural, I commend you. You are a freaking warrior, and you can pretty much do anything, back to the birth plan. We plan, and then life happens. As my due date got closer, I got more swollen by the day. My blood pressure was getting higher and higher, and at a routine checkup, they were concerned about how high my blood pressure had gotten. They had me lie down in a dark room to see if it would go down. Thankfully, it did, but they wanted to make sure that the baby was not in distress. So they hooked me to a fetal monitor. He was doing great, but they wanted to check him once a week. So once a week, I would make the trip to the midwife center and take a half-hour break, lying on my side with this monitor hooked to my belly. Each time, the baby was fine—thank God for that. My swelling kept getting worse. I wondered how long I would be able to work; I wanted to work up until my due date so I could have a longer maternity leave. But when I looked down at my feet during the middle of a work shift, the sides of my feet spilled over my sandals and nearly touched the floor. These were beautiful tan leather Michael Kors sandals. After the pregnancy, I couldn't even wear them because they were so stretched. I knew I might be on my way to an earlier leave. That day, I had an appointment; she brought me in and took my blood pressure. She said, "This is way too high. Lie down, and I'll check it again in a few minutes. If it doesn't go down, I'll have to admit you to the hospital." Once again, it went down—thank God again. She asked me if I was put on bed rest, would I really stay in bed? She said if not, she will need to admit me to the hospital. So naturally, I said yes, who wants to be in the hospital for a month? No offense to you wonderful nurses and health care professionals, but you get no sleep in the hospital, not to mention the germs floating around that place are no joke.

I called the salon and let them know that I was going to be on bed rest, then as I made my way home, I thought to myself, *What will I do for a month, in bed?* I can only sleep for so long; if I knew how much sleep I would get once the baby was here, I might have enjoyed it more than I did. I came home and got into my pajamas. So there in my bed, I sat. Jeremy was working massive overtime during this season of life; I was alone at home for most of the day. I don't mind being alone, but the boredom sat in quickly; I have a hard time sitting still. Over the next few weeks, I found things to fill my time. Jeremy surprised me with a box set of *ALF* DVDs—I mean, who doesn't love *ALF?* When I was a child, my mom would bribe me to eat my dinner by saying, "ALF will cry if you don't eat." So I would sit there and eat to keep ALF from being sad.

I would read books and copied recipes and dreamed about what life would soon be like. I was more than ready to have our baby. I was extremely swollen, miserably big, and bored out of my mind. My two pups kept me company and were my saving grace; my pug Stella and my beagle/terrier mix Maxx never left my side.

Chapter 15

Hey, Baby!

We had to give our little guy an eviction notice; he was nice and cozy and wanted to stay put. So they set a date to start the induction. I waited and dreamed and waited some more. Then finally, it was the day to go into the hospital. I craved Red Lobster during my pregnancy, so naturally, we went out for one last meal as just us. My stomach was so full of a baby that I couldn't eat much, but it was a nice time with Jeremy. He was so nervous that he could hardly stand it; I was so ready that I could hardly stand it myself. That night he took me to the hospital, I got settled into a room. It was a very slow process. It began about ten at night; they inserted a pill into my cervix to soften it and induce labor. The next morning, my water broke on its own; they waited to see if my labor would progress. It did not, so they started Pitocin sometime later in the afternoon; this stuff is awful that I have no words for it. I don't know what regular labor pains are because I only had Pitocin, but it was intense. Now, remember, I still wanted to have no epidural. My midwife told me that I should get one since we were going to need medication to move the labor along. I said no, but took half a dose of Numabine, which barely even touched the pain.

One of my nurses was the sweetest; she was so attentive and kind. But when I am in pain, I just want to be left alone. I need to zone out and deal with it how I do—by going inward and closing out the outside world. This sweet nurse kept asking me, "Are you okay? Doing okay? How are you?" every five minutes. The truth of the matter was I felt like I may die from pain, and there's no feeling better until I have this baby. I didn't want to hurt her feelings by saying, "Shut up!" So I decided to get away. I had a labor room with a Jacuzzi tub. One of my birth plan ideas was to labor in the water; it's been known to help with the pain. So I got up and went to get into the Jacuzzi. The sweet nurse tried to help me, but I told her I was fine and wanted to be alone. I had kept the lights off, and I sat down in hot water and laid my head down on the side of the tub; I was staring out the crack of the door and looking at the light coming in. Then I hear, "Are you doing okay?" You guys, she was in the darkroom with me, and I didn't even see her come in; I'm pretty sure she was a part ninja and part nurse.

Jeremy's work was insane, and he could only get a couple of days off work; I wanted him to be with the baby and me, so I told him to stay at work and call him when the labor started to progress. We were about there; I got out of the tub, and the midwife said that we needed to up my Pitocin. Since my water broke, I couldn't labor for too long without any progression. So she upped it, and the pain got worse; I had my mom call Jeremy, and he was on his way. I had gotten back into the tub, trying to find any relief I possibly could. I sat in the tub until Jeremy came. I wanted to run from the pain or dull it in some way. I was at my breaking point and was ready to cave and get an epidural. I let the midwife know, and she said that she would get that lined up. The pain was getting worse by the moment; I was getting sick and shaking. A thought that actually went through my mind was, "I wish someone would knock me out with a skillet," you know, the heavy-duty cast-iron ones. That makes me laugh now, but I would have seriously taken a skillet to the head. That must be the Southern girl coming out if that's what comes to mind during a time of extreme pain.

Then Dr. Diddy came in and hung the moon. For the record, he's highly recommended by me. He said, "Now I'm going to be putting a needle in your spine. You will feel the needle, and I need you to stay still. It's going to pinch a little bit." Feeling that needle in my spine was welcomed because it took my mind off the labor pains. Sidenote: Things I thought I would never say: "Please stick a needle in my spine." I felt like a million bucks and soon went to sleep for a little while. I was running on very little sleep, and the pain had depleted my energy. After a little rest, I woke up, and I had dilated quite a bit; it was now time to start pushing. Very soon, we would meet our little boy, and the anticipation was running high. After laboring and pushing for a while, his heart showed signs of distress. My midwife told me that they would need to go another route if I didn't have him soon, which meant a C-section. This was the very last thing I wanted to happen; the thought of going into surgery scared me, and the recovery was not something I wanted to go through. If you are reading this and have had a C-section, I commend you. You are a rock star. You are stronger than you know. So I said a prayer; it went something like this: "Jesus, I have no strength left. You have to help me." Then one push later, Jackson Charles Rose came into this world at 10:08 p.m. Jeremy, and I instantly burst into tears; the tears came from a place of joy and from a place of relief that he is safe and from gratitude that God gave me the strength to give that final push that we all needed. They laid him on my chest, and he stuck his arms straight out like Superman, then pushed himself up and slowly and shakily looked from left to right, then he started to cry. It was the most pitiful cry, not a big scream like "I'm so mad." It was more like a whimpering cry; I suppose if I was in a warm dark safe space then had been stuck in a tunnel, a.k.a. birth canal, for hours then was pushed out into a bright cold room, I would be a little sad too. The joy was ours, and we loved that baby more than words can explain.

It was about a couple of hours before we got settled into a room; once we did, Jeremy went straight to sleep, and I lay there in that bed feeling exhausted and like I had been hit by a Mack Truck. There was a slight glow in the room from some sort of small light. Jackson was in the portable crib next to me, and I was just looking at his precious face, then he started to cry. I wondered, *What in the world I do? I don't know how to do this.* Then I just picked up my sweet baby and held him, fed him, and watched him as he watched me. His eyes were so alert, and his little expressions were so quizzical. It was almost like, "Oh, you're the voice that I've been hearing. It was you all the time, Mama." He slept off and on for a couple of hours at a time, and I was so grateful for adrenaline. My heart swelled with love, and I just kept him lying on my chest. I was finally a mom. That was something that I have wanted to be for my whole life. I was now a wife and a mom, and my life felt so complete.

We were showered with flowers and visits; so many people came to meet Jackson. I loved nothing more than showing off my new treasure. Each time someone came in, my face would beam with pride as I would hand my little bundle of joy over them. After two nights, we got to go home. Bringing a newborn baby home is about as nerve-racking as trying to get through airport security.

We get home, and it's dark; we carefully carry Jackson inside, as though he is a fragile egg. I remember thinking, *Where do we put him?* We got the Boppy Pillow and placed him inside, and then we all sat on the couch. This is now how we do life with this sweet little boy. As first-time parents, with a fragile little egg sitting next to us, we sat there on that couch; we started to learn how to transition into the next chapter of our life. Nighttime came, and we got ready for bed; we put him in the bassinet next to the bed, and we closed our eyes and quickly faded off to sleep. Then after what felt like five minutes later, Jackson started to cry. I quickly jumped up and picked him up. I changed his diaper and fed him; he was happy again. If that baby is happy, then everyone is happy. Then just a short time later, he woke up again. Now I haven't really slept a full night, going on the fourth night, and I pushed a human from my body. I would get up with him every couple of hours. My eyes were swollen and puffy, and my brain was so foggy. In my mind, I thought, *This will get better. He just has his days and nights mixed up.* Night after night, it was the same thing. Poor Jeremy was already getting up at four-thirty every morning for work, and being a delivery driver, he needs to be alert and have a sleep, so since I was home on maternity leave, it was up to me.

During the day, Jackson's level of discontent only grew worse. I was breastfeeding, and I realized that I was not producing enough milk. He would eat every hour or two and still was not satisfied. So I called my midwife; she said to hold on, and the production will get better. I chose to supplement the formula; then, he got a horrible rash. In hindsight, I believe he had a sensitivity to dairy. This rash looked like a road rash on his poor little bottom. It was so bad I couldn't even pat his bottom as I rocked him. So this was the new routine: I would wake up every hour, and after forty-five minutes to two hours, I would change his diaper. Due to the rash, I needed to rinse his bottom in the sink, air-dry, coat with Aquaphor, put a soft piece of cloth on it so the diaper wouldn't scratch his rash, then breastfeed until he was so angry and upset from not getting enough milk that he was about to hyperventilate, then I would go make a bottle of formula, hook myself up to a breast pump to keep working on milk production, feed Jackson the bottle of formula; he would chug it and pass out into a milk coma. I would lay him down and then do it all over again in less than two hours. I was drowning; all I could think was, *What's wrong with me? Some women can do this so easily, and I am royalty sucking at this. All my life, this is all*

I ever wanted, and I can't even handle it. What kind of woman am I? What a jerk I was to my old self. I am sorry I let myself think that way. I don't know about you, but I can be very convincing to myself. What I tell myself enough, I'll start to believe it, good or bad. Day after day, the colic and crankiness were present, and I was just feeling worse and worse. One day I needed to take Jackson to a doctor's appointment, and when I got there, I barely remember driving there. I started to feel despair and such exhaustion that I just wanted to cry. Never once would I have judged someone who had postpartum depression, but I just didn't understand how I could ever be sad when I would be living my dream as a mom. I love this little boy more than anything in the world, and all I wanted to do was cry? What was wrong with me? I must have been broken or something. This sounds so silly to say out loud, but it is worth all of the vulnerability that I have opened up about if this even reaches one person.

So now I was thinking about how in just a few weeks, I had to go back to work; I couldn't even take a shower every day, and now I was supposed to pull myself together and all on another huge thing—a full-time job? I felt so defeated and overwhelmed; I felt as if I barely had the strength to get through the day. I had no idea where the strength to leave my baby and do a great job at work was going to come from. I felt like a failure; my silent dream was always to be a stay-at-home mom. I just knew that I was always going to be a second-rate mother because I had to work and that Jackson would have a second-rate childhood because his mom worked. He would have to have the store-bought cookies and store brought valentines for his class—you know, the ones that aren't even close to Pinterest worthy. With the crappy valentines and the crappy cookies, that would be me doing a crappy job being a mom. I would bring my crappy cookies into the school and see the other stay-at-home moms; if you can't tell, I was so jealous of them. I hate being jealous; it's not my normal to feel that way. I am one to cheer on the woman next to me, but this one just got me. But I was so jealous of them. So, back to the story.

I envisioned myself bringing in the crappy cookies or crappy valentines to school and being around the stay-at-home moms with matching outfits and beautiful makeup. At the same time, I look like roadkill because I am so exhausted and defeated and ashamed I was going to fail my son. It hurts to write that; that was a very dark place for me. Possibly one of the darkest t times of my life. I love this little boy with every ounce of my being, and I truly felt as though these things were true. Thank God this was not reality, but it sure felt like it.

Maternity leave ended, and it was time to go back to the salon. The night before my first day back to work, I moped around the house and packed everything I could possibly think of for Jackson. I even packed nail clippers and a brush. I went to bed that night with a feeling of doom and woke up with a stronger feeling of doom. Today was the day that I had to let other people raise my child. Today is the day my failure will be free for all to see. Today is when my second-rate mothering starts; I felt like I was walking the plank. My babysitting situation was actually wonderful; my mom and dad and my sister from another mister had him, then I worked on Saturdays, and he was home with Dad. So I wasn't leaving him to the wolves; he was loved and safe. I just wanted him to be with me, but that wasn't going to be my story. I was going to have to live my plan B life, and so did Jackson; he would have to eat his crappy cookies because his mama failed him.

Chapter 16

A time for change

Most days, I would cry the night before work and cry on my way to work. This was pretty normal for a while. I would call to check on him as much as humanly possible. I would put on my makeup and fix my hair; I would squeeze my postpartum body into stretch pants because I had too much pride to wear maternity clothes, and my prepregnancy clothes would mock me as my jeans would hardly slide past one thigh. My body was a wreck, my mind was a wreck, my hormones were crazy, and I had to pretend that I was doing great. That was exhausting, so hard and exhausting. The salon that I worked at was great for the most part, but they micromanaged me like crazy. I do not like to be micromanaged, I am a self-motivator. When someone tries to treat me this way, it is counterproductive, and that is not an environment that I prosper in.

One day I was having a particularly hard day missing Jackson, and he was only about ten minutes away from my work. I had an appointment canceled, and I asked if I could take a break and go see Jackson. They told me no, they said I needed to stay and wait in case a walk-in appointment came in. Maybe it was the hormones, maybe it was a touch of postpartum, maybe it was the exhaustion, but that day, something inside me snapped. The next day, I went to a local salon and talked to them about renting a booth there. They gave me some information, and I decided to make a move. This way, I would be my own boss, make more money so I could work less, and I could juggle my schedule around Jackson. I could plan around class parties and field trips, and just maybe, I can make some homemade cookies and not have to just have the crappy cookies.

Isn't it funny how sometimes it takes a really hard situation to push you to make a move that will change your life? Well, this was the push I needed. I had all the negative voices in my mind telling me, "You are only as busy as you are because people like that salon. They bring the people in. You have to work harder to do as well as the other stylists." Mind you, this was all lies. Lies that came from a place of poor self-esteem and feeling like I needed to prove my worth. I pushed through; I went home and talked to Jeremy about it, and he was on board, as he always is. He is so supportive of me. Life with me has been a roller-coaster ride of "Oh no, Alicia has an idea." That's how I see it, at least; I'm totally speaking for him. Nevertheless, I straightened my crown, prayed hard, and made a move.

> Dear old version of me, the version of me that was overweight, depressed, stressed, and in total despair—the version of me that actually thought that working moms couldn't bake homemade cookies,
>
> Guess what? Working moms bake freaking amazing cookies too!

To the version of me that thought being a working mom was a bad thing, a thing to be ashamed of, who thought that it was living my plan B, who thought that Jackson would have a second-rate childhood because of it (I'm talking about that version of me):

> I am giving you a hug right now, and I am so glad that you got to the other side of that.

I am so glad that I can tell my old self that I am proud to be a working mom. I am a freaking amazing mom. I am an amazing wife, and I am happy. The old version of me wouldn't have ever believed that. Can anyone relate to me? What if you went through the hard things you went through just to show others that you could move the mountain? Moving the mountain in your own life gives you the credibility to show others they can move their mountain too.

Dear old version of me,

You can show others how life was not in your favor as a small child, and things were often hard growing up, and you still pushed through and persevered. You don't make excuses to play small and be mediocre. Yes, you make mistakes along the way, and you fail over and over again. But you failed your way forward, and you didn't stop. Think about how you are struggling now. You are depressed, tired, and you feel like a failure. You are paralyzed by what people think of you. The very thought of someone not liking you crushes you and sets anxiety in. You are a people pleaser, and you have to have come to a crossroads—do you please yourself and your family or people in the cheap seats? You know the answer to that. You're about to upset many people you tried to please by doing this move, but you now know this is your time. This old version of you is now falling away. You are outgrowing your old self and are stepping into a new journey and a new version of yourself. I know this because I am you seven years from now. I hardly recognize you. This is the start of a whole new journey in your life. Can you even imagine what you could accomplish if you were in a healthy state mentally and physically? You would be unstoppable, freaking unstoppable. Keep going no matter how hard it is. Your breakthrough is just past your breaking point.

I needed to buy myself some time to get my clients in order, so I started talking to them when they were in my chair, and for clients that I didn't see in person before the move, I found their phone numbers and reached out to them on Facebook. I got a Square card reader to accept payment, got a picture taken for business cards, and purchased a few bottles of retail products to sell, along with hair color and back bar products. Then just like that, I was an independent stylist renting a booth at a new Salon. There was just one last thing I had to do: tell my old salon that I was leaving. This was a very hard thing; the thought of it made me shake, made my stomach twist in knots, and I really didn't want to do it. I was ready to leave but not ready to have them so upset and face the confrontation. Another stylist at the Salon Rouge that I was friends with was also leaving to rent a booth at another salon. If one of us told the salon first, the second one would surely have a harder time telling them, so we decided to tell them together. We both had the same day off. We met early in the morning in the parking lot; she got into the car with me, and we sat and waited for the salon manager to pull in. If we told her in the salon, we would have no privacy and didn't want to make it any more uncomfortable for her or ourselves. I saw her pull up, and I knew I had to drive over to her, and my foot would not push the gas pedal. I was so scared, so freaking scared. But I did it. I pushed the pedal and drove over to her. We got out of the car, and she asked if we were out running errands. We told her we were leaving. I saw her get teary-eyed, and I hated it. We didn't want to hurt anyone or make anyone upset, but we had to do what was best for our families and us. It was awkward, so very awkward. But we did the hard thing, and we survived.

We went out for breakfast at Bob Evans restaurant. Jackson was with us; he was such a little thing. That little guy gave me the push I needed to make a move, a move that would end up changing the trajectory of my family's life but in the meantime, made some people pretty upset with me. Isn't it funny how dads always know what to say? I was telling my dad that I wanted to go independent, and he said, "Wouldn't you have to have zero self-esteem to not do that?" When he said that, it gave me clarity; I don't even know if I told him this, but that simple sentence gave me the strength to do this thing. The salon I was moving to remind me of the Greek Parthenon. It was very beautiful, filled with sculptures and marble tiles and pillars; there were a ton of stairs. It was a very large building, and it had a lot of stylists inside; it was two levels, and there were stations back-to-back. We had a common area where we would mix colors, and nearby was our lockers, where we would store our hair color and other supplies. This was my start, a place where I could be a boss and make my schedule. Making the leap from "being guaranteed to make some sort of paycheck" to "only making a paycheck if you could make your business work" was a bit unnerving. To my surprise, I was able to make a whole week's paycheck in about a day; the first day I worked, I was walking out to my car in disbelief. It would have taken me a week to earn this much money. Being driven to a fault helped me out this time. I have to say that I never worked harder in my life; being independent means I shopped for supplies, I booked the appointments, I handled customer service issues, and of course, I did the hair. I was in charge of my education, my everything—and I freaking loved it! This gal was no longer being micromanaged, and

I knew I was on the right path. Learning how to book my appointments with timing took a little doing, and I have to admit I messed that up a few times, and that was stressful, but I figured it out; I kept going and kept making mistakes across the board. After a while, I got the hang of it, and it became a lot easier. Now I can do it in my sleep; what once was hard and took a lot of energy now is just as natural as brushing my teeth. I had changed my schedule to work two twelve-hour shifts, an additional evening and Saturday. I got to be home and raise Jackson and even make cookies. I was making more than enough to help support our family, and all was going well. It was strange to want to go to lunch and just go; I was so used to asking people for permission to do anything.

This was very liberating. This gal was no longer being micro-managed, and I was spreading my wings. Things were not perfect, but I had not liked the way my life was going before—how I was going to have to work and the amount of time I was going to have to be away from my son. How I was told when to work, how to work, and then being told what I was worth being paid. I decided that I was going to have enough confidence in myself to push through my discomfort to get comfortable. It was like I was walking down a staircase, and I could only see one stair at a time. If this gives you a little tug at your heart, and you are thinking, "Wow, I really wish I could do this thing." or "Wow, I really wish I have a life that would allow me to do this." or "Wow, I really I want to work from home." "I want to start a business." "I want to start a blog." "I want to switch careers." Sister, I'm talking to you; you got this!

About six months into working at the new salon, I felt very comfortable running my own business. I started to wonder what it would be like to have my very own space. Not only renting a booth. There was a building of suites that was near completion. It was a large building with individual suites inside. They were rented out to salon professionals. The rent was just about the same as what I was already paying, and I could have my very own space. This sounded like something I was interested in. I contacted a leasing manager, and he showed me around. I was sold almost immediately. I had a few months of my contract left by the time that I had gotten all of the details around to make a move. I was overjoyed having my own space. I got to name it, pick the wall colors, and decorate it however I wanted to. I had twenty-four-hour access to the building, and it was brand-new and very pretty. The only downfall was the size; it was very small. Of course, I went with the smallest space at first to be cost-effective. It had enough room for a styling chair; there were built-in cabinets, and I had two small brown parson's chairs and a teal circular table. It was so pretty; I just loved it. One wall was magenta, and I had put a gold stencil design on it; the other three walls were teal. The curtains were a gold color with a design on them.

Mom helped me so much; with everything going on in my life at that time, my creative energy was spent. My plate was full, working at my current location, preparing my new space, and having Jackson being a year and a half old. I showed the mom colors I liked, and she put the ideas together and helped me shop. During that phase of my life, I was still finding my decorating sense. So it didn't all come easy to me. She helped me pull it all together. Once I was ready to move, I let all my clients know. I have to brag on my clients for a minute. I have the absolute best clients I could have ever asked for. Many of them have been with me through the moves, and we have become friends. We have laughed together, cried together, and know more about each other than you could imagine. So naturally, they were very supportive and were excited to see the new space.

It's pretty traditional to have two clients in the salon at one time; that's how I had been booked at the first salon; that's also how I booked at the second salon. This space was too small to do that, so I would only book one client at a time. After a while, I grew accustomed to the space I had, and it felt amazing to have a space to call my own. The size was difficult, though, so after a year, a larger corner unit came available. It was of course, more expensive, but if I moved into this space i could double book and it would make up for the extra cost of rent.

So I talked to Jeremy about it, and he was supportive as usual, so off I went. I moved right down the hall. I had about double the space, and it was great; I had a larger area for chairs, so now I could double-book. This was great for about a year, but I had no windows; I had never had a window at Sola, and I really wanted to have a window.

Guess what happened a year later? Yes, you guessed it. I moved once again. Right up to the front of the building, and I had windows on one whole wall. I had even more space. It was so pretty; I had a mini couch and a white TV. I was coming into my own with my decorating sense. This time was easier for me, but yes, my mom still helped me. I had white walls and Lucite furniture; the mini couch was a cream color. I had a Lucite table with a mirrored top and accents of gold. I had tripled my space, my rent, my clientele, and my confidence in three years. Things were growing and scaling very fast.

It was about a year into my stay at the window front suite, and I was so very content. I thought I would stay there forever. I loved how the building was run; I loved my space, and all was great in the world. Then I was getting into my storage closet one day, and things started to fall out. I had outgrown my storage space, but it was not a big deal. Nothing is perfect, and I have nowhere else to go. I have the largest suite in the building; I have all of the beautiful windows, I have everything I've wanted. Then I truly believe God put this desire into my heart: "What if there's more, what if I dared to dream? What if there's something else?" Then I thought, *I finally got my beautiful windows. I hate to leave this beautiful place.* Then not long after, a woman I had recently met was telling me that she has her own shop; it was just down the road, and it was much less expensive, and she had a lot of room. The location was *amazing*! I had to say I was curious. *This is crazy*, I was thinking to myself.

I started thinking about it and praying about it; of course, I talked to Jeremy about it, and he was on board. I talked to my parents, and they were also in agreement that it was a great idea. So I sat on that for a very short time, then guess what I did?

Chapter 17

God Gives Us the Desires of Our Heart

I contacted the leasing manager at the new place that I was interested in; I just wanted to look at some spaces, get an idea of the leasing price, and see what kind of construction would be needed. So I made an appointment; it was a couple of weeks out, and I started a Pinterest board with salon ideas. If this did happen, I wanted to be prepared. I pinned ideas with white walls, a rustic-wood-looking floor, and industrial hardware shelving. This was my vision and my dream. I had worked alone for some time now, and I missed being around other stylists, so I wanted to rent two chairs to another stylist and have a nail tech take care of our clients.

These buildings that I was looking at were built the year I was born, in 1985; they were very clean and kept up, but they were not remodeled inside unless a previous tenant had done so. In its prime, this was the place where you wanted your office to be, but lots of people moved in and out over the years, and it was hard to guess what type of building would be available and what decor and flooring it would have. Most of the buildings needed remodeling, which was what I was preparing myself for. There were so many variables in this and so many unknowns, I decided that I would trust God, and whatever He did for me was what I wanted. The day came when it was time to go see some spaces available. I got to meet the leasing agent. I was there for a while and was waiting, and she never showed up. I thought that was my answer, but I called the other leasing agent just to touch base. I wanted to make sure that I didn't mistake the time or anything. He answered and called the other leasing agent, and she called me and let me know that she had forgotten and that she could meet me shortly. I was fine that, and I waited with much anticipation.

She pulled up, and we chatted for a moment, then we went to look at the first property that she wanted me to see. I kid you not; it had white walls and a rustic floor; it had so many windows, more than my other location. The whole front was windows; there were windows on both other sides of the room, and as if that wasn't enough, there was a waiting room that came with space; there was nearly a whole wall of windows! I dared to dream, and then this happened; it was amazing. Now what happens next is even more amazing. I asked what the price was, and it was nearly half of what I was paying, and the space was about five times larger, and it had more windows. Right outside the front door is a big tree, and there are birds and squirrels, and it's so peaceful.

So I tell her, "I really want this. I need to talk to my husband and show him the space. Can you give me a few hours?" She said, "Yes, of course. She let me have the key to bring him in and see it." Then I asked her about when I could move in and such. I let her know that I was under contract with at my current location. I asked if she could hold it for me for a few months, then I could just overlap payments for a couple of months. She looked at me and said, "You know what, I can tell you will be a good tenant. How about if you sign a long lease. I'll give you six months' rent-free. That way, you don't have to be stressed with the overlapping rent payments and moving." I was in shock. Who does that? God was blessing me and paving the way before me. I was so humbled by their kindness and, most of all, the blessings and kindness of God. He was giving me favor and creating a way; He was creating a way for me and my mom as well. I'll get to that shortly. So I thank her over and over again, then I get into my car. I'm weeping. God drops dreams into our hearts; if we trust Him and hold His hand and walk in faith, He will lead us. If we are a good steward with little, He will give us more. He cares about the little details; God cared about what was on my Pinterest board. He led me to a place that had more windows than I would have dared to dream of, let alone ask for, and the walls were white, the floor was rustic-wood-looking, and the lady that had the space before was a stylist. I worked with her at my first stylist job; she already had plumbing done for a shampoo sink.

When we pray, let's pray that God will bless us according to His riches, not our own. Our minds can't even fathom all the blessings that God is willing to give our loved ones and us. If we would only ask, let's not play small or pray small. These are a few scriptures that have really helped me. I challenge you to write these on a place where you will see them often, like on a notecard by your bathroom mirror, where you will see it every morning. Or even on your mirror. Keep it on your desk at work or in your wallet, maybe even in your car.

> You have not because you ask not. (James 4:2)
>
> Ask, and you will receive, and your joy will be complete. (John 16:24)
>
> And my God will meet all your needs according to the riches of his glory in Christ Jesus. (Philippians 4:19 NIV)

Let's go boldly before the throne. Let's ask and expect miracles and blessings in the precious, perfect, and powerful name of Jesus. Did you know that when you go to God in the name of Jesus, He sees us as He sees Jesus? This is so because Jesus died for our sins; His blood covers our sins.

I called my mom. I said to her, "You will never believe this." She asked me if I got a pixie cut; we had been talking about getting a pixie cut. I've never been brave enough for that, even though I find them to be so beautiful. For those pixie girls out there, you rock! I laughed and told her no, then I explained what had happened. She was as awestruck as I was. When Jeremy got home from work, I explained everything; he said, "Yes, *go* for it!" So that's what I did. I took him and Jackson out to see it, and they both loved it.

Now I needed to set up a salon; this was a new thing for me. I had worked at a salon, rented a chair at a booth rental salon, and rented a furnished studio, but I've never started from scratch. So here we go. Jeremy was such a help in all of this; we sat down and talked about everything that I would need to get started. We needed stations, styling chairs, two shampoo bowls, a retail shelf, decor, more seating, a regular sink, a color room, and shelving for the back bar.

We got to work. Jeremy started looking online and ordering; as things would come in, we would load them up and drop them off at the new salon. We made our industrial shelving from raw wood and made our shelving brackets out of metal plumbing (thank you, Pinterest). We stained the wood, and Jeremy hung the shelving. Jackson was the one who picked up all the packing material that was floating around and kept the floor swept. This was truly a family affair; when our work and the school day were done, we would go to the new salon to work. Little by little, it all came together.

The maintenance man that helped manage the salon property put the stations together for me. Those stations came in about five hundred pieces; I hope he has forgiven me. I never thought to measure the wall space when we ordered the stations; it was another miracle because they fit perfectly, and there was enough elbow room to not be squished.

We got everything put together, and it looked so beautiful. Now I wanted to fill the two extra chairs. So I put up a post, and immediately a friend messaged me and said she wanted it; and shortly after, another one chimed in. So just like that, Studio R was born. It was only about three minutes from my prior location and things switched over seamlessly—well, almost seamlessly. All of the buildings looked exactly alike, so for the first six months or so, I had to stand out by our big tree and wave people down; after a couple of appointment cycles, it's smooth as could be.

Now I had wanted a nail tech. I thought it would be amazing to have a nail tech there to take care of my clients while they process or before and after appointments; it would be an instant clientele with two other stylists there. I had talked to my clients about it, and they absolutely loved the idea. Now I had to find a nail tech. I had reached out to a nail tech that I knew, and she was possibly interested, but she had a full clientele. This wasn't going to help me out at all. I needed someone right out of school. So my wheels were turning, and I started to think of ways I could figure this out. Then one day, I was at the new salon with Mom, and we were looking out the big window facing my favorite tree, and I said out of nowhere, "Mom, why don't you quit your job, go to school for nails, and be my nail tech?" I literally don't know where this came from. I had not been thinking about Mom being that person.

She quickly laughed and said, "No, that won't work. It would be nice, but I need insurance."

I let that thought go as quickly as it came. We started talking about something else, and the day went on as usual.

The next morning, Mom called me really early, around 6:00 a.m. or so. I quickly answered, assuming something was wrong; she sounded so giddy and then proceeded to ask me if I really meant what I said yesterday about her working at the salon. I responded,

"Yes, of course." Then she said, "I'll do it!" I couldn't believe what I was hearing; she probably couldn't believe what she was saying—this was amazing. It was going to be a blast.

Mom had been very discouraged with her current job. She was a cake decorator in a cake factory-type setting. The hours were exhausting, and the job was very physically demanding; it wasn't just decorating pretty cakes and cookies; it involved lifting fifty-pound buckets of icing and squeezing icing bags until her arms and hands hurt. She had to wear wrist supports at night because her hands were numb from carpal tunnel syndrome. Her body hurt, and so did her emotions; although she loved some of the people she worked with, she did not like that job.

We all know that if we feel stuck in a job that we don't like, it's depressing and can be downright miserable. That's where she was: she was miserable. I had no knowledge of this, but a couple of months before I started to think about opening the salon, she prayed a prayer that I feel put these events in motion. One morning she was very tired, discouraged, and wasn't sure how she was going to keep going in the direction she was. She stopped and stood by her dresser and prayed a prayer that went something like this: "God, I can't keep going like this, I see no way for change, but You can make way for me."

What if I was also standing by cabinet at my old salon at that exact moment, and the idea dropped in my mind that I would like some more storage; what if that little idea was placed in me because He was answering her prayer. That idea got my mind thinking about change; even though I was perfectly happy, God had bigger and better plans for my family and me.

A rising tide lifts *all the boats*. (John F. Kennedy)

I can honestly say I did rely on God through this whole process, and He removed obstacles for me; He made what could have been hard and scary fun and exciting. Following God is not boring and mundane; it's an exciting adventure. I must tell you, though, the worst thing that I can do myself is start to reason. What God places in our hearts may not make sense in our heads. I'm not saying act irrationally or anything like that, but listen to Him and don't reason it away if you know that God is calling you. When we get that feeling that we just know God has something for us to do or is calling us into something, that is called discernment. I also believe that God will place little glimpses and desires into our hearts to keep us excited and motivated to move forward; sometimes things take a lot longer than we want them to, and we must keep our eyes on the prize and stay in

God's timing, and not take things into our own hands. I've done this, and it will quickly turn into a mess. God's timing is perfect.

Next week, Mom and I went to Vogue Beauty College, where I attended cosmetology school. I knew most of the teachers and directors there, so I got to introduce her; she signed up for school that day, and I took her picture. How the tables have turned. It was so much fun. She was planning on going to school part-time and working part-time; it was going to take twice as long, so I encouraged her to quit her job and go full-time. It would take three months full-time and six months part-time. I was so ready for her to be in the shop with me that I wanted to move it along. She wasn't ready to do that, and I understood; she didn't want to leave her friends hanging at the bakery—her work ethic is solid. I would go into the school and get a Pedi or mani and visit. One of my favorite teachers was now Mom's teacher; her name is Miss Lisa. She became one of Mom's favorite teachers as well. After a few weeks of working and school, it was just too much. She took a big step and quit her job to pursue school full-time. In just about two and a half months, she was done—just like that. She passed with flying colors, had a new trade under her belt, a new career to look forward to, and she had made a ton of new friends. She truly cherished the group of people that she met at school. The best thing of all was that we got to work together! On her last day of school, I met her, and we went out for lunch at a place called Jesus; of course, it's pronounced different being a Hispanic restaurant, but I feel it's still a wink from God.

She was embarking on a new journey. She was her boss as she was self-employed, and she was now going to make her own hours, wear pretty clothes and shoes; she didn't have to even think about a uniform, and all this was the ripple effect of prayer. When she prayed that prayer, she believed that God heard her and that He was going to help her. I believe that she had no doubt in her heart. She took one step without seeing the rest of the staircase, and I am so proud of her. She doesn't have ever to miss another holiday dinner, another family function. She is free—free to build the life she dreams of.

She quickly grew a clientele; my clients and the clients at the salon loved her instantly. Many of them said they felt like they already knew her because they knew me so well. It makes my heart so happy; it was just a short time in that she was already making her old paycheck and surpassing it. Also, she no longer had carpal tunnel issues and has no fear of wearing ugly nonslip shoes. The tides were rising, and the effects were trickling onto every part of life. Jackson got to have more Nonny (that's what he calls her) time, and my dad gets to have his wife back, and I got to work with my mom!

Chapter 18

Alicia Rose's House of Curl

When I was a teenager, I read a book called *Patty Jane's House of Curl*, written by Lorna Landvik. This was the very first book that I read on my own just because I just wanted to. Of course, I read books in school, but reading for fun was not in my normal daily activities. This book sucked me right in. It was about a young married couple; the woman was pregnant, and the husband wasn't sure how he felt about it. The husband leaves one day and never returns. She is left to raise their daughter on her own with the help of family and friends. She decided to open a little salon in her home to support herself and her daughter, and of course, she calls it Patty Jane's House of Curl; she endures hard times but keeps going and even has fun along the way. She told stories about her life as a "hairdresser"; it was so good. There is a real twist at the end; I won't spoil it if you decide to read it. It was about half my life ago, and it's still imprinted on me. As

I'm writing this, my phone beeps; it was a text message from a client. It said, "Good morning, I just need to stop what I am doing right now to send you a text because I always think to send you a note to tell you how much I love my haircut. Thank you so much!!! I hope you have a wonderful rest of your day! See you soon!!" This melts my heart. I guess I have my very own House of Curl, which I am so grateful for. Patty Jane's House of Curl supported her family, and my House of Curl supports mine.

It also supports my desire to make other women feel good about themselves, to build them up, and help them talk through their problems. Mostly just listening and asking them questions, sometimes that's all we need, just to talk and not have someone try to fix our problems or tell us what we're doing right or what we're doing wrong or getting mad at the person you're upset with. Sometimes it's just a neutral person that listens and lets you talk out your issue. Sometimes I feel that we can have a huge scenario built up in our minds; it seems so dark, terrifying, and horrible. Then when we say it out loud, it doesn't seem so big, or there are simple solutions that could be applied, or possibly the problem isn't even real, just a creation in our mind that's filled by our fears and insecurities.

Our minds can be harder to train than a defiant puppy. Our minds—well, at least my mind does that. I'll sit down to write, and suddenly I feel the need to make sure I messaged someone back or check to see if I mailed out that bill, or I'll think of a recipe to google. I have to constantly stop and bring my mind back to what I am doing. Multitasking is a myth—there, I said it. To multitask is to do a bunch of things, frankly, not very well. I've learned that to be a fact in my life and am always working on being in the present. Doing one thing at a time, and doing it well, being all in. If I'm talking to you, I want to be with you and listening, not daydreaming about going for a run later or what I'm going to make for dinner. If I'm at home, I want to be 100 percent at home; if I'm at work, I want to be 100 percent at work; if I'm on a date with Jeremy, I want to be 100 percent with Jeremy on that date. If I'm visiting my parents, I don't want to be answering text messages. If I'm reading a book to Jackson, I want to be right there with him 100 percent reading the book and using the funny voices and watching him enjoy the story. Our people are just too important; they deserve our full attention when we are with them. You get the gist of it: a busy, noisy mental that is pulled in multiple directions all the time is not a healthy mind state to be in. It can cause anxiety, depression, exhaustion, and just being downright overwhelmed. We must be fully intentional about what we fill our minds with and how much we fill our minds with; if everything is important, nothing is important. Choose what fills your mind and schedule wisely. To be completely truthful, I am always working on this and failing; I just try to fall forward and acknowledge that I had fallen, then intentionally set my intentions again and again and again. I've come a very long way in this area and have a very long way to go. I am okay with that; I am—and we all are—a work in progress, perfectly imperfect, and walking and falling our way through life. I certainly don't have it all figured out, and I'm okay with that. I hope you can give yourself the grace to be okay with yourself on your journey, loving yourself even when you mess up and not throwing in the towel because you make one mistake or maybe ten mistakes. It's okay, and beating ourselves up only hurts us more. So once again, fall forward and land on a cloud of grace, love, and self-acceptance, and remember, Rome wasn't built in a day. Got it? Good, because you are amazing, and there isn't another like you.

The salon is now full of life and fun. Mom is there working hard right alongside me; the days are spent telling stories and laughing. We have a friend named Sean, a massage therapist, who works down the hall in the same building; our goal is to see how bad we can scare each other. We share a space in the basement where we have a washer and dryer; it's dark and a bit creepy down there.

Sean was walking down the stairs, and I was doing laundry; I heard footsteps and hoped it was him. I hid behind the door and jumped out, and scared him. I truly feel joy in scaring people; that may make me a total weirdo, but I'm not changing my ways. We laughed and laughed; laughing is medicine. I feel that a day that we haven't laughed is a day wasted.

There is never a dull moment, and it's safe to say that this would not be our reality without a prayer, a dream, pushing through during the hard times. Do you have a dream that you know God is leading you to, but you don't know where to start, or maybe you are frozen with fear or swimming in a sea of doubt? I wish I could reach through the screen or the page and hold your hand and tell you that your dream is on the other side of the mountain. Right on the other side. Mt. Everest can't be climbed in a day. Most likely, either can your mountain. But each day, if you take small steps, they will add up to long-lasting change and have you closer and closer to your goal. Sometimes there are days, weeks, or even months when I'll stop and think, *Is all this hard work worth it? Will it ever pay off?* Then usually, right around the corner is my breakthrough; I'll get over that mountain. There is always another mountain, and while we are in the valley, it is hard to see where we are going; it's hard to deal with discouragement and doubt. During those times, set your gaze straight ahead and put one foot in front of the other and keep slogging along; soon, you will be at the mountaintop looking back, thanking yourself that you did not stop when life got hard because if you would have stopped, you will still be stuck in a hard place.

Sometimes we have to decide what kind of discomfort we want. Do we want the discomfort of being uncomfortable in our skin, our jobs, our heads, or do we want to do things even when we don't want to or do things scared? Taking the first step of faith will activate God's plan for you. One step at a time; we don't get to see the whole picture. We see what is right before us; we can trick ourselves into thinking that we can control the future and keep ourselves safe if we plan enough. That is a lie that we tell ourselves, and it gives us a sense of false security. Where is our security supposed to come from? It's not our status, job, money, family, abilities, or accomplishments. It is supposed to come from God, and when it doesn't, we have to scratch and fight trying to keep it. I have tried this, though; even if I wouldn't have admitted it while I was going through it, but dang it, I've walked down that path, and it is hard, exhausting, and downright discouraging. Trying to keep something that was never meant to be ours. We must take a narrow, long, and requires much faith to get that best version of life. But what you leave behind is great; you get to leave behind guilt, worry, shame, fear of the future. Can you imagine what life would look like if you unpacked these things and didn't put them back in your bag? How light would that feel? How would you act, treat your spouse and your family? What if you quit juggling and decided that you want God's plan, not your plan? What if you could heal?

I challenge you to stand up and take a step toward the life you deserve. I can promise you that it will be unpredictable; it will be uncomfortable, but isn't life already that way at times? When you step into the life that God has planned for you, amidst the times of discomfort and unknown, you will be fulfilled, you will be excited and passionate, you will be healing, and anxiety and depression will fall away. I am not talking about true mental disorders and chemical imbalances, even though I believe that God can heal anything in our minds, bodies, and souls. The result of a true imbalance is not your fault, and you can't think it away, but there is help, and God will guide you in the direction that is best for you. He heals through many ways, including doctors, medicine, and right thinking. Have you ever been sitting around and feeling so sad or discouraged? Have you ever stopped and thought about what you're thinking? We have control of our thoughts. I've been guilty of this many times: I would be thinking about all the what-ifs in life until I would be so discouraged and sad that I just had no energy left. What we think about matters. You will not feel guilt or shame for not living up to your potential and fret over the future or what lies before you.

For most of my life, I have been a slave to fear, a slave to other people's opinions of me, a slave to not measuring cup, a slave to people-pleasing, and a slave to achieving. If I could achieve all of these things, I thought I could earn my worth. Many years ago, I read this verse; it was my dream. I didn't know what life would look like when I got there, and I didn't care; all I knew was I would chase after this.

She is clothed in strength and dignity, and *she laughs without fear of the future*. (Proverbs 31:25)

This scripture painted a picture of a version of me that I wanted to be; this was biblical, so I knew this was available to me even though I was buried with fear, anxiety, and depression. Even though in my mind it was hard to convince, my spirit knew better. My spirit knew to keep on when my mind said, "No, play it safe." I pictured myself happy and able to enjoy my family and friends while not worrying and having fear; this version of me was confident and happy with a contagious joy. I wanted to be her and have that life; the cost to have that kind of life was the life I had then. Talk about trading a purse from Dollar General for a Louis Vuitton bag. Even though trading my old life for a new one was a no-brainer, it was still really freaking hard. It was hard because, as humans, we like to know what will happen and how things will play out. It feels easier to stay in our pain, misery, and bondage because at least it's familiar. Having made it to the other side, I can safely say your feelings will lie to you, and they will also trick you. You have to decide that you will move forward, no looking back, getting up when you fall, and above all else, don't doubt yourself.

If you accept my challenge and you're going to take the first step of faith, let me say this: just as you are, flaws and all, you are *worthy*, you are *good*, you have *value*, you are *irreplaceable*. In my life, I had realized that I could never grow, create, or heal when I was coming from a place of lack. Will you take a moment and get into a quiet place and close your eyes, think about the hard things you have overcome, the things that you have walked through. Think of the very hardest thing. Maybe it brings up some hard emotions, and that's okay; you can begin to work through them. Now think, if you are reading this, then you are still alive. You still have a purpose on this earth. You are stronger than the thing that tried to break you, ruin you, or kill you. You overcame that thing, and you may have scars, but that is nothing to be ashamed of; that proves you won.

Think of the things you love about yourself; and about what you are proud of. If you think that you have made too many mistakes or that you are bad for God to use you or want to heal you, then please hear this: our God is a redeemer, a healer, and a restorer.

He wants to restore what you have lost; He wants to redeem you and your life. He wants you to have an amazing life on earth as well as eternal life. You were bought with too high of a price for Him to cast you aside. The Bible is full of people who were the lowest of the low, such as prostitutes, idol worshipers, tax collectors, and even the apostle Paul who was killing and persecuting Christians; and God took them, changed their hearts, and used them to make history. God doesn't use the worthy; He uses the willing; if you are willing, He is able to change your heart, your mind, and your circumstances. He can open doors and create opportunities that you never dreamed possible. Are you willing? If so, take a moment, find the love that you have for yourself, and know that you are enough, and you are only going to get better and unearth a version of yourself that is already inside of you; you have to excavate her or him. Start this process of healing and restoration from a place of self-love and trust that God is now leading the way. I must say, by no means am I a licensed counselor; I am not; I have no formal training, but what I have is what I have experienced and what God has done in my life and before my eyes. I am proof that you can have a different life; I am proof that you have freedom and joy in life. My life story is my credential; each of our stories is different with a whole different story and different problems.

I wish I could tell you that this would be easy, but it's not. I don't want you to think that there are no more hard days and trials because you are trusting God. Trusting God and walking through faith is not an easy road, but it's the best road; it's a road filled with peace and joy and daily giving your worries to God, over and over again. It's making mistakes and getting back up; it's not quitting. I don't want to set you up for failure thinking you're doing this wrong because your problems don't go away instantly or that you fall back into old ways; you probably will. But just get back up, ask God for strength, and do it again. Have you ever seen a baby trying to walk? They try to walk, and they have those shaky baby legs, and they try so hard, then they fall over and over and over again; the mother doesn't get mad at the baby because the baby can't walk well, the mother cheers the baby on and picks them up and wipes their tears away. We're the baby, and God is the mother—well, in this case, the father. If you keep getting back up, before you know it, you will be off and running. In the coming chapters, I'm going to share some tangible advice on how I overcame a lot of my obstacles. Some you may reside with, and some you may not; just take what works for you, and leave what doesn't. I'm cheering for you!

Chapter 19

Determining What Your Goals Are

How do we chase after a goal if we don't know what the goal is? Good question, right? I did this for years: I would hope and dream of being happier, more confident, smarter, healthier, and when I stopped to think about it, what does this mean? I had to break it down; for instance, if I were to put that list into tangible goals, it would have said, "I wish to be free from anxiety, confident about the way I look, confident in my skills to write a blog, book, and run a business, and be in great physical shape." Do you see what I just did there? I made a vague list of wishes into a list of tangible goals. I would wish for each thing; I put the true meaning of what I actually wished for and gave it its name.

1. Free from Anxiety

For each goal, I made a list of what it would take to achieve this goal. For instance, (1) Free from Anxiety. Sidenote: As I had mentioned earlier in the book, I had struggled with anxiety and had a few panic attacks in my life; it was hard, scary, and it felt as though it was stealing my joy, and to be honest, some days it did. It would rob me of being present with my family and friends because my heart and mind would be racing, and I could barely keep my train of thought. I took anxiety medicine for a while and stopped and had to get back on it. When I started writing this book, I was taking it. I wanted to stop taking it before I started writing this, mainly because I felt like a fraud—how could someone like me, who has to take anxiety medicine, write a book and help anyone at all? See how silly that sounds? Our inner jerk, as I like to call it, can be so mean. There is nothing wrong with taking anxiety medicine, but I knew it was a Band-Aid to a deeper issue that I had to work through in my case.

Writing this book has brought me so much healing. I quit taking medicine a few months ago. I did it cold turkey, and I do not recommend that; it felt awful, the symptoms lasted a few days, but I am free from the medicine and the symptoms that came with taking it and the symptoms that came with the withdrawal from taking it.

I decided that I would do everything in my power to be free, and I prayed so hard, I drank chamomile tea, but guess what? I had to face my junk, my ugly garbage, and I had to put it into the light. That's exactly what I did with this book; as I started writing and cringing as I would type the details of the story that I wanted to pretend didn't happen, something changed. The overwhelmed and exhausted part of me from trying to pretend to be okay started to fall away. Simply because I admitted that I was not okay, that gave me the freedom to heal. Starting from the very beginning and thinking about each year of my life to put it into words dredged every raw emotion out of me; it picked every scab and forced me to face my fears of being judged. This book has been my therapy; having finished the life story portion, I can see that writing was a beautiful mess of emotions, and I am so glad I did it. If this book even helps one person, it was worth it all. I have to say writing this book helped me more than I had ever expected. Something really cool happened when I started writing this book and was open about it; people asked me what it was about, and I told them. That was so uncomfortable at first, but then it got easier and easier, and now it's not a big deal at all to talk about. I suppose if I'm going to put this out into the world for everyone to read, I better get comfortable talking about it. The more honest I was, the more honest other people were with me;

they opened up about really hard personal issues. When we allow ourselves to be vulnerable, it permits other people to do the same. What if we could live in a world where we spent our time and energy growing and owning our life instead of spending all of our time and energy trying to cover up how we really are? I believe that is possible. It can start with just one person, and they can rub off on their circle of influence. Do you think you don't have any influence? Well, my dear, I say this respectfully, but you are wrong. Do you have a spouse, child, parents, siblings, coworkers, a grandparent, a person that bags your groceries at the store? I'm sure each of you has at least one of these. Your influence on your circle. Have you ever noticed how a person's energy can change a room? For instance, let's say that everyone is in the break room at work is enjoying their lunch and chit-chatting, then Negative Nancy comes in and says, "My lunch is not awful, I wish I would have ordered food." or "I'm so tired, and this is such a bad day." Now Negative Nancy has changed the conversation to negative things, and it's easy to take the bait; if you do, then the whole room gets that negative vibe. The version of me that started writing this book and the version that is writing this chapter is quite different. Her bag is a lot lighter, and that old junk that I had shoved so deep down inside is now gone. I had to let that heavy load go. I have healed and became closer to the person that I want to be. I'm a lot closer to that Proverbs 31 woman, who is clothed with strength and dignity and laughs without fear of the future. When she speaks, her words are wise; and she gives instruction with kindness. If I can, then, my dear reader, you can too.

2. Confident

Back to the list, (2) Confident. I had to think about exactly what I didn't like about myself. Sadly, that was easy. It is simple to pick out our flaws instead of finding things we love about ourselves, isn't it? I didn't have to ponder that for long; I knew the answer. I didn't like my weight; the extra thirty pounds I have been carrying around for way too long just needed to go. Sadly, it's still there; although I am a lot healthier than before, I still haven't managed to lose the pounds. This was also a thought that I wanted to conquer before I wrote the book. I wanted to give a long list of all the things I had overcome and be a real inspiration. The only problem with that is I wanted to have overcome every issue that I've dealt with. This, my reader, is not reality; this is not real life. We can be in the thick of an issue, and we are still worthy. If I had waited to write this until I was perfect, then it would have never been written, never read by a soul. Just alphabet soup floating around in my brain. So if this is something you deal with, in any way, remember, as my great-grandma Mary said, "Life is not a dress rehearsal." Again, we are living life right now, and if we try to be perfect before we take any action, we won't take any action. Perfection is a lie; it's an Instagram filter, not real life.

This issue went hand in hand with my first issue, anxiety. I was a comfort eater. I used food to feel better when I was anxious, sad, stressed, and tired. I worked through that problem, discovered a healthy, sustainable eating plan (goodbye, yo-yo diets, and cycles of eating everything followed by eating rabbit food), and know that I am on the path to shedding those unwanted pounds. But deliverance often comes little by little, just a little here and there; for me, it's often two steps forward and one step back, and you know what? That's okay, I just keep stepping and falling, but I fall forward; even if I fall, I'm still a little farther ahead. For instance, our family had had a cold that keeps circling around our house; no matter how much bleach I use, it just won't die. When I didn't feel well, I often lost all of my willpower, and then as if I needed to make things any harder, I made corn soufflé. You guys, it was so warm and bubbly and sweet; it was so good. And I ate more than I should have. I kept going back for more bites straight from the pan. I woke up feeling very bloated and disappointed in myself, but then I said to myself, "Wait, I'm not going to feel guilty all day and beat myself up. Yesterday's mistake does not get to bleed into this day." Then I packed my lunch for the day and made it extra nutritious, and I was going to chug water like it's my job, and yesterday's mistake will not have power over today.

In the past, I would have kept going; my inner dialogue may have sounded something like this: "Well, you really screwed that up, might as well have whatever you want and start fresh on Monday." This may sound so silly to some, but I know some of you will get me on this, and, sister, we have to stop this. We can't keep going through this cycle. Today, make a choice that you will stop; you will give yourself grace, and when you make a mistake, you will speak kindly to yourself and fall forward with me. Fall forward and get back on track. Remember what we tell ourselves. After a while, we will start to believe. Believe good things about yourself.

So to feel confident, I needed to get at a healthy weight; I needed to go into my closet and have my clothes fit. I have always loved clothes and fashion, and now my fashion choices were being dictated by what stretch pants were clean. Sisters, this is no way to live. I want to dress according to what I feel like wearing, not what will stretch over my thighs. Anyone with me here? Also, clothes shopping has been zero fun for a long time, and a-rockin' outfit makes me feel confident, not overworn stretch pants. I was stuck in a cycle of clothes that did not make me feel confident, and I had decided against buying one more pair of stretch pants. I will not accept that for my life any longer. I also needed not to see a muffin top; nothing spilling over the top of my pants was acceptable either.

3. Smarter

My third goal was I wanted to be smarter; when I really gave this some thought, what this meant was I was afraid I would not be able to achieve the dreams that I have inside my heart because I wouldn't know how to execute them. My dreams are pretty big and audacious, and I was afraid that I was going to out-dream my ability. PS: God calls the willing, not the worthy. If God gives you a calling, He will open the right doors and give you all you need to succeed; it may be resources like Google or a podcast, maybe a friend who had gone before you and knew how to achieve that goal that you are calling. He has many ways to help us, and He never runs out of resources. I now pray every day for God to bless my family and me according to His riches.

Are we ever amazing at something for the first time? Usually not. There may be a person here and there who can nail it the first time, but new things take some work for me. When I had the dream to write this book, I had no clue how to write it, and calling myself an author or writer just made me giggle. Could this be reality? I didn't know how many words I needed to have in the book, how many chapters, how to get a book published, I didn't know how to do any of this. But I did know that I had to get these words on paper; I had to tell my story. Guess what helped me? Google. What would we do without that Google search bar? We can find just about anything we need to help ourselves on the Internet, and most of the time, you can get it at no cost other than your time. YouTube is also an amazing tool; there are so many people who are willing to share their skills and wisdom. It's a great resource to take advantage of. So I needed to figure out exactly what I wanted to be smarter and read, listen, and learn about that subject voraciously. That is just what I did. I know how to just accept that there are a lot of things that I don't know how to do, but I also know that those things won't stop me. I will learn a new skill as often as I need to continue my growth journey and to follow any dreams that may drop into my heart. I must add that another lesson that I learned was "just because I can do something doesn't mean that I should." Not all things are worth our time and energy, and some things should be passed to another person; for instance, building a blog was completely mind-boggling for me, and I did not have the desire to learn how to do this. So my amazing cousin did it for me. She is a computer programmer and website designer, and I think her so much! You are amazing, Laurie; I love you, cuz. So using discernment on what to take time to learn and when to hire or what to ask for help with will help you not to waste time and move forward more quickly.

4. Healthier

My last goal was to be healthier. I wanted to be in amazing shape. Not just so-so, but in such great shape that I could be confident in front of people even if I was wearing a tank top; I wanted toned arms and a lean body. I also wanted to feel amazing, like spring out of bed at 5:00 a.m. bright-eyed and bushy-tailed. I wanted to have all the energy, but I also wanted to eat junk food and sugar-laden cookies. Food is our fuel, just as gas is fuel for a car. If we put bad gas in our car, we can't expect it to run properly. The same goes for our diet. My diet was mainly good, but adding in junk food regularly was very normal for me. Especially after 8:00 p.m., when the day is done, and Jackson is in bed, Jeremy and I sit down for the first time of the day, and we have our time to talk and binge-watch a few episodes of *Stranger Things* or old reruns of *Roseanne*. It's our time to be together, and what goes with great conversation other than some snacks like chips and salsa or cookies. And guess what goes with chips, salsa, and cookies? That darn muffin top that I wanted to lose. It's interesting how that one thing, emotional eating, has woven its way into most areas of my life. So I needed to trade some not-so-good habits for some better ones. Like hot tea, I got a variety of teas—some detox tea, sleepy-time tea (be cautious not to drink too much green tea before bed—learned that the hard way). Also, bubbly water; if you like carbonated water, this is a great addition. I have three varieties in my refrigerator right now. I never run out of bubbly water. I also put a nice hand lotion on the end table. I'll sip my tea, bubbly water, or sometimes a nice glass of red wine, and then when I'm done, putting on my hand lotion keeps me busy, and I forget about the chips, salsa, and cookies. Replacing habits is easier than just stopping a habit. Having a better replacement is easier for me to ease into something; it may also help you.

That was my list of goals. What are your goals? I challenge you to get a pen or pencil (my fave) and jot down the thoughts you have when you "wish you were different" or you wish this or that. Write them down and make a list of your wishes, narrow them down to a few, then put some thought into them. Ask yourself questions like, why do I wish this? Then ask yourself why, again and again, as many times as it takes to get to the root of the thing that you wish for. Then when your list is written out, write a definition next to the word of what you need to pinpoint and tackle. For example, "I want to be happy." I may ask, what is making me unhappy? And go from there. There is no wrong way; we just need to deconstruct and get to the root of what we wish for so we can make it a reality. You also now have a list of exact goals as opposed to a list of wishes. Goals can be achieved through hard work and persistence; wishes don't happen that often unless you are one of the lucky ones who have won Publishers Clearing House or have a personal genie. I don't know about you, but I don't want to live my life by chance and spend my days waiting and wishing. I want to determine my goals and work toward them. If you're reading this book, I bet it's safe to say that you want to take charge of your life too.

Once you have that step completed, get some knowledge on how to do the things you need to do; maybe you want to become a pilot or go to med school. Ask for help, google, read books, talk to someone who has already accomplished the thing that you want to do. Then write down tangible steps that you will need to take to start working toward your goal, things that you can measure. For example, while writing this book, I kept track of my word count. That way, I can measure my progress by how many words I have written and how many I need to complete. Remember to keep it simple and don't give up.

Chapter 20

Make Up Your Mind

Now that you have an outline of your goals and start looking for knowledge and advice, you will be bombarded with information coming from all directions. A lot of it contradicts something else that you just read. You can spend hours and hours scrolling for advice and ideas on Pinterest, but until you stop looking outside yourself for change, you won't have any true lasting change. You know what you need to chase in your heart, so make up your mind what you're going to do and keep your mind set. Do not waver. They say if you don't stand for something, you will fall for anything. Make up your mind, set your mind on what you will do, and then get information on how to do that thing. I have wasted so much time circling the mountain changing my mind because, in the back of my mind, I decided what I wanted to do was going to be too hard and be too much work. So I try to make myself think I can be happy with something else or doing something else that's easier. In the end, we already know what we need to do; we know the answer. In the end, the wavering was just a waste of time; time is too valuable, and we only have so much, so use it wisely.

There will be days that seem to drag on forever, and it may seem that your hard work is not paying off, but keep pushing. Find a way to measure how far you have come. You may even be able to remember a time when you prayed, wished, or dreamed of being where you are now. Don't take that for granted. You're on your way. The biggest goals I've ever accomplished were by talking small diligent actions every single day; it didn't even seem like I was getting anywhere because I was inching along so slowly. Like a snail, but then one day, you look up, and you are on chapter 20 of a book you dreamed of writing. Today was an aha moment; small diligent steps are what change your life. Being persistent is not easy, not with most things. Persistence is going on that run when you don't want to; it's when eating the salad when you really want the cheeseburger—and you've had a long day, and you feel like you deserve it. Persistence is not rewarding yourself with something now that is not a reward for your future self. Now onto another subject.

The state of my house is the state of my mind.

Let me ask you a question, what does your house look like right now? What does your car look like? What does your purse look like when you take a look inside?

If it's full of unorganized mess, it's safe to say that until you get that cleaned up, you may feel discombobulated and overwhelmed. I always say to myself that the state of my house is the state of my mind. I like clean, organized, and in order. Then when life throws curve-balls, I don't have to wade through stacks of paper to find my sanity. I have a calm, clean place of refuge. Of course, we have daily messes, and there are superheroes strewn all over the house and spaghetti sauce splattered on the stove sometimes, but we try to clean up the messes and keep the order in our home. For us, it's a family affair; we each do our part, and with Jackson being seven now, he has his responsibilities, such as cleaning his room up before bed and putting his laundry in the hamper. Jeremy does the laundry, and I keep up with the kitchen and bathrooms. Don't get me wrong, sometimes things get out of hand, or it's a super-crazy week, and things get messy and out of order, and I feel it. Mentally and emotionally, it drags me down, and I despise it. I know that not everyone has a spouse to help them, but just do the best you can with what you have. For me, I've experienced that less is more; if there's an area of your house that keeps getting cluttered, and you have tried organizing it, and it's still a mess, try getting rid of some of the stuff. It sounds so simple, but it's not always easy; the freedom that comes with it is huge, though.

Another thing that has been extremely helpful for me is simplifying our cooking and meal prep; also, if you're really busy, Shipt and Instacart are amazing. It's an app where you order your groceries online, and they are delivered to your door within two hours. The service is $100 a year, and I have to say I've saved well over $100 a year in impulse buying and coffees to drink while I'm browsing the grocery store. It also frees up time to work on that list of goals or just have a break. There is no additional fee per delivery as long as it's at least a $35 order. In this day and age, that's easy to reach that amount; add milk and bananas, and you're there—okay, I'm joking, but you get the idea. Another thing that I really love to do is plan out freezer crock pot meals. Its very simple and you can find so many recopies online. It's also very cost effective.

Back to the meal prep. On Sundays, I like to have a grocery order delivered. Then I'll clean veggies and fruits, chop them up. I'll put them into containers for easy access to throw a salad together. I'll cook some fish and place it in a glass container with a lid and a lemon in it to help keep it fresh. I don't go over three days just to be safe. I'll boil some eggs, peel them, and divide them into containers to grab and go. I have a shelf in the fridge for Jackson's snacks; I stock applesauce cups, baby carrots, string cheese, and I keep a bowl of fruit on the counter. I try to keep healthy choices available to everyone; there's no easier way to set ourselves up for failure than being hungry, and there are no healthy choices ready to grab. Then I try to do at least one meal that we can eat for two days, such as chili, a hearty soup, or spaghetti. My best advice would be finding the right rhythm for you and your family, trying things, finding what works great, and reworking what does not. This, too, should be a journey that is always evolving; it should be a joyous journey.

We are coming to the end of our book journey together, and I hope I've thought to tell you everything that I can think of that may help you along the way. The journey is long, but it can be so glorious, scary, hard, fun, crazy, fulfilling, and freaking amazing. I hope that you dare to dream, then I hope you dare to turn those dreams into goals, then I hope you make it a reality because while you are on your path to fulfill your dreams, remember that you started worthy; you don't need to reach for that. You start worthy; you are good how you are, you are irreplaceable and amazing, you are enough just as you are. I hope that you love yourself through your journey and enjoy the ride. I'm rooting for you, sister!

About the Author

Alicia lives a simple life with her husband, Jeremy, and their son, Jackson. She believes in putting family first; following that is her passion for helping women overcome their past so that they can create the life they dream of. After walking through many hard situations herself and overcoming them, she aspires to ignite the desire in other women to choose to do the work and not settle for less than they deserve. Each woman deserves to live their best life, and their past has absolutely no power over their future course. As women, we are resilient and strong; and when empowered, we are unstoppable.

CPSIA information can be obtained
at www.ICGtesting.com
Printed in the USA
BVHW082340210322
632055BV00001B/45